A MEMOIR

George Rowley

ORIGINAL WRITING

ISBN: 978-1-906018-02-3

A CIP catalogue for this book is available from the National Library.

Line from Patrick Kavanagh's The Hospital reprinted from *Collected Poems* (Allen Lane, 2004), edited by Antoinette Quinn, by kind permission the Trustees of the Estate of the late Katherine B. Kavanagh through the Jonathan Williams Literary Agency.

CONTENTS

To my wife, Kathleen, whose love and support have sustained me for the last forty years

ACKNOWLEDGEMENTS

There are many people without whose support I would not have been able to write this memoir. I wish to acknowledge them all. In no particular order they are:

Mary, who typed the manuscript—how she read the manuscript I do not know. Her editing skills were also crucial. Also my publishers, Original Writing Limited—Andrew and Martin Delany.

Listowel Writers' Week under the chairmanship of Joanne Keane-O'Flynn; Eilish and Máire from the Administration Office; Madeline O'Sullivan, Máire O'Connor, David Browne, John McGrath, Bill Walsh and Sheila Barry from the Committee.
   Bernard Farrell, Fintan O'Toole, Christine Dwyer-Hickey, Nuala O'Faolain and Jack Harte whose workshops I attended at Writers' Week over the years.

Dr. Matt Murphy and Mara DeLacy from St. Patricks Hospital, Dublin.

The management and staff of the Gresham Hotel—Toddys and the Writers' Bar—under the direction of Mr. Derek Duggan. The management and staff of the Skylon Hotel, Dublin especially the three Pauls.

Mrs. Mary Keane and Billy Keane, Mr. and Mrs. Donie and Mary Costello.

PART ONE

1943–1950

I ALWAYS THOUGHT THAT MY PARENTS were the only victims but I was to discover in later life that I was a victim too. I have been in many dark places, helped out of them by kind psychiatrists who knew what they were doing and tons of various types of medication, which seemed to work. Being in touch with reality is a painful business but I have survived and feel grateful as I reach the final stretch to the great beyond—that is the end of a life—mine. But isn't life a gift.

But back to the beginning. I came into this world, such as it is, on 22 September 1943 in Holles Street, Dublin where all the country women had their babies. I was the third of seven children born to George and Nora Rowley, nee Gallogly, who hailed from County Leitrim.

We first lived in a rented artisan's cottage in Upper Grangegorman off the North Circular Road. 86 Orchard Terrace was the address my mother liked to use, as it seemed to her grander. The back wall of our house was the side wall of St. Brendan's Grangegorman, the public Mental Hospital where I was to spend some time in 1969 but more of that later.

Upper Grangegorman was to me a grim street and all the artisans' cottages were owned by Willie Sheridan who had a garage at the junction with the North Circular Road. Willie was a decent man despite his wealth and was a widower and had a housekeeper named Sally. My mother often expressed regret that Willie did not marry Sally ever. I think my father paid rent of £1 per week for the cottage. My father was a carpenter, a very skilled one and even at the height of the war, he always had work—though I remember once seeing his passport in a drawer, which he had ready in case he needed to go to England for work, which it transpired he never did.

To my memory, the cottage consisted of one bedroom where we all slept. There were six children in 1948. There was a sitting room for visitors and there was a kitchen and a scullery with a toilet out in the backyard, overlooked by the intimidating grim wall of "the Gorman", a name it is still known by today. Now, what do I remember of this humble abode over sixty years on? Firstly, I never recall being hungry, never in my life have I felt hungry. I remember the neighbours. The Hennerty sisters, Mary and Hannah, who had never married and who had been milliners and were in their seventies. They lived in just one room. The Doyles lived in one room also across the hall from the Hennertys. Mr. Doyle was a waiter in a posh hotel in the city but was reputed to be fond of the drink and gambling. They had one son, Michael, who when he grew up, joined the merchant navy and settled in Australia. I was to meet him in the 1960s and often had a pint with him in the Hut down on the North Circular Road in Phibsboro. The Doyles never owned a home of their own, as far as I can recall.

Next to that cottage where the Hennertys and the Doyles had lived—a miserable existence, it seems now—lived the Murphys. He was a guard and she always seemed to be on the verge of hysteria—laughter of children seemed to upset her. I can only remember one of their children, Bobby, who was to get a job in a chocolate factory. Many times he gave us chocolate.

Next cottage was the Kavanaghs and then the Rocks. One of the sons, Jimmy was reputed to be wild when he got to be a teenager.

The Gleesons lived next to the Rocks and a son was to become a priest but later left his vocation, and married a native African, which gave rise to a scandal in those bygone days of innocence. There lived a severely mentally handicapped girl, Breda Hickey, in the house next to the Gleesons, and she never left the house, went to school or anything like that. She looked out the window all day and wonder always got the better of me as I passed by, frequently looking into her impassive face through the eyes of a very impressionable child which conditioned me to what I was to become on the torrid road to now.

The Egans lived in the next cottage—they hailed from Offaly and wanted the best for their children, two boys Michael and Ciaran, as my parents did. He was a hardworking barman who later saved enough to buy a pub in James' Street and a house in Connaught Street, Phibsboro which was then regarded as prosperous. We were more friendly with the Egans who went to O'Connells School, North Richmond Street where all the three Rowley boys went after the convent. But my brother, Joe, first went to St. Canice's.

So this was Upper Grangegorman, a series of rented artisans' cottages where I grew up in the forties. I remember the wonder of the ration books, which I discovered in the drawer in the sitting room. Across the road were the purchase houses styled Orchard Terrace, which began with a lane, running down from Devlin's Garage. Maud Perdissat, a spinster civil servant, lived in the first house and was obsessive to a manic degree in keeping the whole place clean. Maud was constantly at war with her next-door neighbour, Mrs. Moynihan from nearby Stoney Batter who was married to a guard from County Kerry and as I recall they had nine children. She always called him Moynihan, to his chagrin. They were all girls except for one boy who later joined the Special Branch, having tried carpentry but failed at

3

that. My mother was very friendly with Mrs. Moynihan, who always seemed to be looking for tea or sugar from her in those war years. Joe, my elder brother, remarked one day, "What does she want now?" when Mrs. Moynihan called to our door. I am trying to recall now the names of the Moynihan girls, Nora, Helena, Catherine who went as a novice but came out of the convent before she took her final vows. Margaret, a big friendly girl—but that is all I can now remember. Mrs Moynihan always seemed to be baiting Maude Perdissat in her frantic efforts to keep her place clean. Maude worked in the Special Employment Schemes Office and when it closed, she joined the Office of Public Works where I was to start in 1963. She used to say to friends, later when I would meet her in the Gresham Hotel, "Georgie and I grew up together." One year in the OPW, Jack Walshe, a great and kind mentor of mine—who was then a Commissioner—asked me to chaperone Maude to the Office party. I did not chaff one bit for I can say, modestly, I was and still am capable of great kindness. It seems natural to be kind when you have been in pain yourself. I was to join a handful of mourners at Maude's funeral when she died in her eighties, years later. As a child, I was in mortal dread of her, as she would puncture our balls if they happened to go into her well-kept garden. She would have been regarded as a harridan when I was a child in the forties but when I got to know Maude when I joined the OPW I thought she was gracious and kind but very lonely. In the sixties and seventies, I would regularly join her for tea, at her request, in the Gresham or indeed the Shelbourne. If she was proud of me and, I feel now she was, she was prouder, even still, of her brother who achieved high status in, I think it was, the Department of Education. He predeceased Maude and she never got over his death. Maude was of an older bygone era and would have regarded herself as a lady.

Down Orchard Terrace lived the Dohertys. Mr. Doherty was in the Free State Army as my father derisively called it and they had a large family. I was very friendly with Joe in the sixties and we often drank in the Hut. He was a mechanic in Devlin's garage but later became a security man in Securicor and I was asked by the Company for a reference. Joe was worried because he thought the word would get out that he was in the IRA or at least on the fringes of it at that time. I recall, with pleasure, many evenings sitting in one of the lorries in the garage with Joe, full of Guinness, and eating fish and chips, innocent were the pleasures then. The Burkes lived next door to the Dohertys. I think there were two sons, Sean and Paddy. Sean was in and out of hospital, with what was euphemistically called, his nerves in those days when mental ill health was regarded as a stigma and only spoken about in whispers. Even as an adult, Sean suffered badly.

Then next door came the Ryans and I remember Una, one of the daughters, most of all. She was very friendly with my sister Mollie and would wear you out talking even to this day. But she seemed joyous and free of baggage and if I would meet her now I would not try to avoid her though, as I said, she would talk for Ireland. Then came the Sherlocks and Mrs. Cunningham. Further down was Devine's sweet shop and there were two sons and a daughter, Mick, Paddy and I think Reeney. Across from the Devine's was the grim, remorseless wall of the Gorman about fifteen feet high on its way to the main gate. Further down on the left from Devine's was what we called the Grippo, which was a wall with holes in it which enabled one to climb to the lane which ran from Devlin's Garage. It was reputed that the Grippo got its holes from bullets during the 1916 rising which I often discussed in the 1950s with Mary Hennerty when I would bring her milk and sugar. She had been born about 1880 and I loved, even at my tender age, to talk about the old days when she said Cabra was an orchard and the now Charleville Road, off the North Circular Road, was just a lane. My father in 1952 fulfilled the dream he had been saving for when he bought a huge house on the New Cabra Road for £1,750 cash, but more of that later. I am still in the forties and am down at the Grippo, which is still there. The street then merged with Rathdown Road, then regarded as very posh, and the Muldoons, the fish people, had a house there. I became friendly with Aideen, one of the girls when I was burgeoning as a man in the late fifties.

As you go further down, the main gates of the Gorman are on the right, with the old clock tower on the left—1816 is still emblazoned on it. At the bottom of the hill, it is right into Kirwan Street dotted with cottages, which now cost a fortune in 2007. A couple of hundred yards on you reach Stanhope Street Convent where I went to my first day at school in 1947, 1948 or thereabouts.

I was told afterwards that I cried on my first day at Stanhope Street Convent and did not want to leave my mother. I was a mother's boy then, though she would have found it hard to give me the attention I howled for as she now had six children under the age of seven. In the early days at the convent, I would often cry to go back to my mother to say a proper goodbye. These were the first signs, I suppose, of insecurity on my part, danger signs, perhaps, of what was to happen years later.

The convent was typical of those built in the 1800s with high ceilings and windows with a garden where the May processions took place, which were a joy to my innocent mind. The nuns were the Sisters of Charity. I only remember a couple of them now. Sister Stanislaus who wore glasses, tinted blue, and Sister Gethsemane, who was in her eighties then. Mrs. Lowry was my first teacher and there was a Miss Dunne. Sixty years on I do not recall much of my early days at school but I remember if a boy was caught misbehaving, he was threatened with having to sit with the girls—the shame of it.

I must have been childish for my age because Sister Stanislaus called my mother down to the school the year I was to make my First Communion and told her that I was too immature to comprehend the meaning of First Confession and First Communion. But my valiant and determined mother fought my corner and got her way. I was to make my First Communion in May 1950 with the rest of my class, to my mother's delight. My mother, who was an expert knitter and always seemed to have needles and wool in her hands, knit me a navy blue pullover for the big day with wine stripes through it. I still have the photograph with my white medallion, black shoes and shorts. I can say now that I looked angelic but everyone does at that age, I have to admit.

I remember the solemnity but what I recall most now is that I lost my mother in the convent garden afterwards and went hysterical; she must have been only out of my sight for a few minutes but it seemed an eternity to me as I wailed. Was this normal for a seven-year old or was it another sign that I was different? But we are all different and aren't we all unique.

I made twenty-five shillings on my Communion day, offerings from the neighbours, tokens of the poor and the pious, sixpences and shillings. I was a rich young boy of six but was mean as hell and would not share the chocolate with my younger brother Gerry that I bought for sixpence in Hoey's sweet shop beside Sheridan's Garage on top of our street. I am glad to say that I am not mean now and when I was drinking, I was a bit of a fool buying drink for total strangers. The brand of chocolate was Cadbury's Bournville and it was very strong.

Even as early as 1950, I was always full of fear and a dreadful sense of foreboding and that I would be punished whether in the right or wrong. I remember an incident in my last days at the convent when there was some boyish messing in the class and the teacher would not let us go home until the culprit owned up. I became stricken with a terrible fear that I was the guilty party though I was not and was about to confess when another boy held up his hand.

The high point of the school year was the May processions through the convent grounds, the weather beautiful and the flowers in full bloom, the hymns *I'll sing a song to Mary* and *Hail Queen of Heaven*. I can still get emotional recalling their beguiling airs and words now. But through a child's eyes and ears, they were a joy, which sustained a belief in God that I have never fully felt since. Maybe it was all a con job, the opium of the people but I, for one, swallowed it hook, line and sinker. The belief in God, a power greater than myself, has never fully left me. Though I have done terrible things and suffered pain, almost unendurable pain for years, I have somehow held on, even by my fingernails, to the concept of a Superior Being.

PART TWO

1951–1960

AFTER HOLY COMMUNION, THE BOYS had to leave the convent and head for boys' schools, mostly the Christian Brothers who had the reputation of achieving good results mostly through tough methods but also a deep knowledge of the educational system. Like most parents of my generation with their working-class background, my parents wanted all of us, including the girls, to have a good education as a platform for a permanent job in the Civil Service or teaching. The other jobs in industry or insurance companies needed pull, my father believed passionately. Stanhope Street Convent was the main feeder school for Brunswick Street Christian Brothers School, which Paddy Crosbie was to make famous in *The School Around the Corner* radio show in the fifties. Micheal Doyle from next door went to Brunswick Street, as did Joe Doherty. But my parents opted for O'Connells School, which had an enviable reputation for results and academic success. My elder brother Joe first went to St. Canice's, a sister school of O'Connells, which was down at the bottom the North Circular Road beside Croke Park. But no easy entry for Georgie, as I was called as a boy. Joe was told by my mother to tell the Principal of St. Canice's, a Brother Curtis, that she wanted me to be enrolled in June 1951. But like any shy boy of that age, my mother discovered that Joe did not approach Brother Curtis at all, either through fear or forgetfulness. So my mother being told this by the Brother, when she brought me down, that he knew nothing about it. That was a fateful May day in 1951, fifty-five years ago as I write this. Brother Curtis, a kind man, suggested to my mother that she bring me down to Brother O'Donoghue, the Principal of the adjoining O'Connells school and see, even at this late stage, if there was room for me. My agitated mother led me down to the monastery at the top of North Richmond Street and we met Brother O'Donoghue, who must have been in his sixties. He told my distraught mother that the entry classes were full for the coming year and after discussing the options, he suggested that I be sent to the convent in North William Street, where I could stay for another year and then I could enter O'Connells in 1952. My mother rejected this out of hand, and even I, shy as I was, emphatically said I would not spend another year in a convent. As luck would have it the Brother relented in the face of our appeals and said I would have to do an entrance exam; so I went into a room beside the hall in the monastery that I got to know so well during my time at the school until 1962, when I was in fact expelled, but more of that later. I cannot recall the details of the test but it was sums and spelling and when I was finished, I handed my efforts to the good Brother and I passed. No doubt my mother was relieved but she said, "Wait 'til I get home to Joe and teach him a lesson."

So that is how I got accepted into O'Connells, the most illustrious school in all of Ireland, for results anyway—and that is how my parents judged it anyway. Boys came from all over Dublin to go to the school, even from as far away as Rush and Donabate, in the North County, and Drimnagh and Crumlin on the fringes of the south city.

I went into 2A, which was presided over by Brother Mullane,

who I was to later meet in my official capacity in 1987, when he was a priest in his seventies. Brother Mullane was kind, nice and gentle. He had a leather strap but I do not remember him ever using it, on me, anyway. The high point of the week was when we had a reading of *Shadow the Sheepdog* by Enid Blyton, and that was when I got my first love of books. There were other books too but that is the one I can now recall. Dermot Flynn was the most popular reader because of his refined accent. My accent was flat Dublin, which my mother regretted, and she enrolled me for elocution lessons when I was in fifth class.

We heard in awe the news of King George VI's death in 1952 but otherwise it had little impact on us, as O'Connells, like all Christian Brothers' Schools, passionately expounded Irish Republicanism. In the Christmas test of 1951, when I was in second class with Brother Mullane, I got 22nd place in a class of about 55 boys. I knew at once that my father would not be pleased, and felt even if you got first place in Ireland he would not be happy. "Aren't you fed and clothed like the best of them," he would say. I hope that I am not doing him an injustice by these remarks but my recollection is crystal clear. He was rigid and hard, that is my memory and I was in mortal dread of him, which conditioned me to what I was to become. Though I admit my fault in it all too. He was remote and unreaching to me as a child and what governed all his actions towards us was that he was terrified that we would turn out badly. This is what made him firmly believing in spare the rod and spoil the child, which he regularly embraced even with the girls. I know my two brothers Joe and Gerry laughed it all off and came out of the experience relatively unscathed but I did not. I am not bitter but I find it sad that it was so unnecessary. I am not saying that the tough regime I was raised in at home and also at school lead completely to what was to happen me but I have no doubt that it was a significant factor. My father knew nothing better than this rigidity; he was raised that way himself on an eight-acre farm in Leitrim. In my view, he was totally unprepared for rearing a large family to whom he was devoted and was proud of, something he kept well hidden. Like us all, he had no precedent for anything but believed hard work, the grind on a building site, would make us all successful by his criterion. Yes, we all achieved material success, but it was at a price for myself and my sisters, Rosemarie and Anne, who all suffered nervous breakdowns. Maybe it was a gene—my mother suffered a breakdown too, about 1940, after she lost her first child and a cousin of hers had frequent bouts of insanity in the fifties and sixties. But the unremitting regime did not help me anyway. As this is my story or at least my memory of it, however flawed, I will only sweep my side of the street. My father said at one time about me, he must have taken the wrong baby out of Holles Street; I was so different, so odd, and so sensitive. That hurt then, but to a lesser degree now. Though my mother said I was very like my father, obdurate and stubborn. In later years after my mother died in 1977, my father used to go with me as an outpatient to the Gorman for depression, which I think was caused by the loss of my mother, which he never got over. Theirs was a silent unexpressed, to us anyway, love. My doctor in St. Pat's said that it would be a mistake on my part to believe they were not happy. The point is it was never expressed openly—in their private moments perhaps. I forgive him now, that silent distant figure, who so dominated my life until he died in 1983. As I have said, I forgive my father and I hope wherever he is, he has forgiven me. I was wronged but I no doubt caused him terrible distress in later years when I was in the process of cracking up—which took eight years before the ultimate explosion in my system brought about by obsessions and alcohol to which I first resorted, to numb the pain I felt in those years.

It was in 1952 that we moved to 75 Cabra Road, a huge achievement for my father. As I said earlier, he had saved £1,750 to buy it. I could not even do that now. The excitement was palpable as we moved in. There was a dining room, a sitting room, a kitchen with a tiled floor and a room at the back of it called the "maid's room", a relic from the days when the house was owned by gentry. We never had a maid; it was my mother who served in that role. Upstairs there were three bedrooms. The one at the front you could play football in, where the three girls slept. Later in 1952, Noreen, the baby, was born and I remember well the morning my mother was taken to Holles Street in August of that year. It was the first time I became aware of the concept of birth but had no idea of how it came about. My mother just went to hospital and a few days later came back with this bundle of joy and joy she was to me. It was I who always rushed to Noreen with a bottle when she cried at night—the boys' bedroom was next to the girls. And below at the break of the stairs was my parents' bedroom with the bathroom beside it.

There was a huge garden abundant with flowers—it was May, I think, when we moved to Cabra Road. The first thing my father did when we arrived was to get rid of the telephone. A man of frugal needs, he never saw the need for such until the family got him one after my mother died in 1977.

One incident I remember from that time was my father shouting at Noreen to keep quiet when she was crying. My mother was a queen in her vast kitchen with its Rayburn fire and gas-cooker and two formica tables, which my father made. While my father was very political, my mother's Republic was her family and her seat of Government the kitchen. All my father's friends had been in the IRA after the Civil War and were unrepentant Republicans and Socialists. Though my father was radical and leaning to the left he never joined the IRA as such, but the house was regarded as a safe house by his IRA friends. Indeed, Ruarí Ó Brádaigh of Republican Sinn Féin confirmed this to me on Anna Livia radio in the mid 1990s. Jumping ahead to the late fifties, John Joe McGirl convened an *Ard Comhairle* meeting of the IRA in our dining room and though he was a sympathiser, my father was not pleased. Indeed, I, who was in my teens at the time, raised objections too. John Joe who was from Ballinamore, Co. Leitrim, where my mother was born, was a lifelong activist—we are still friendly with his family; he promised my father after the meeting a bag of spuds which we are still waiting for until this day. I think what bothered my father was that he was taken for granted, a thing you would do at your peril. Though a democrat all my life, I still think that that band of intimates of his, were great men. They were too young for the 1916 rising and perhaps the War of Independence and they were convinced that the treaty was a sellout and they viewed anyone in constitutional politics as traitors. I can recall most of them now. Leo Duignan, who spent time in prison in England during the war. Paddy Earley, who was a hardline Communist rather than Republican. Mick Ferguson, Micksie Conway, Tommy Reilly and Syl Fitzsimons who was a builder and had a dog called Toss, Hughie McCormac, a fiddle player from Leitrim, like my father, and many more I am sure. From these early days my father, in June, brought the whole family in his car (he had always had a car from 1947) to Bodenstown to the Wolfe Tone plot, the father of Irish Republicanism and we would meet all his friends, mostly IRA men. It was really a day out, especially for my mother who one year, much to her embarrassment was served a half-pint of ale in a pint glass in the pub in Straffan where often fights would break out amongst the itinerants, now called travellers. We would all march the two miles to Bodenstown and I would listen with awe to the orations at Tone's grave. I believed it all then, eyes and ears wide open.

In 1981, I met Leo Duignan in Bodenstown when the hunger strikes were just finished with ten IRA men dead and I asked Leo was it all worthwhile. He had the conviction of a child believing in Santa. He said that the Provisional IRA were the greatest patriots that Ireland ever produced. Leo was a carpenter too, from Leitrim and he spent ten years in jail in England for his Republican convictions. In fact it is a measure of the man that when an amnesty was called by the British in 1947, he refused to take it, as he would have had to sign a bond never to return to England on the grounds that when his mother died a few years earlier, the authorities would not let him go to her funeral, in spite of the fact that he promised to return to jail. His word was his bond. He said in 1947, at the time of the amnesty, "You would not accept my word when my mother died so why accept it now?" So Leo served his full ten-year sentence. When Leo came out of prison, he married Gobnait Ni Shuilleabhain, a native Irish speaker from Coolea, who never seemed to stop talking. Leo was a silent man; he listened with great civility, but rarely spoke. His son, Eoin, is now a famous traditional musician in Dingle and another son, a doctor, died tragically. I went to Leo's funeral and the family videotaped the service. His daughter, Muireann, is well known in Irish Language circles. They were a wonderful family but Leo was a diehard and unrepentant until his last gasp.

As I said, Paddy Earley was a convinced Communist. He was self-educated and a great debater who won many competitions. In his forties, he married Lulu Fleming whose sister had earlier married Syl Fitzsimons; Lulu was much younger than Paddy and they had one son, Breffni, who is now a teacher. When Lulu and Paddy were about to get married, it was said and I believe it, that Lulu went to the priest to try to get Paddy to go to confession before they got married. But he refused. He did not believe in God, not one bit. I remember one Sunday morning when I was about fifteen and becoming politically aware, Paddy called to our house and got out of his new car. I piped up—I was precocious then—I said, "Mr. Earley, how come if you are a Communist you have a car and most working people haven't?" His retort was immediate, "Droppings from the tables of the rich." His smile was huge. Even in his eighties, I would see him picketing Leinster House about some issue or other. One day in 1987, I was going into Leinster House with Mary O'Rourke, the Minister for Education, and Paddy was on the picket-line. I said to the Minister, "You have to meet this man," giving her some of his background. She was very gracious and spent some time talking to Paddy about various issues.

Paddy did not accept Gorbachev's *Glasnost* or *Perestroika*. He

remained a confirmed stalinist and though he had a church funeral at his graveside, there were three different strands of his
life that made up the whole man. The IRA angle with John Joe
McGirl, Trade Unionism and to top it all a decade of the Rosary.
If there is indeed a Heaven, what I wonder did Paddy make of
meeting a God of my understanding?

Tommy Reilly used visit my father on Sunday mornings. His
wife lost a lot of children through miscarriages and when a child
was born to her eventually, it was handicapped, and did not live
long. Tommy was also a carpenter and was always cheerful despite his misfortune. Tommy also did prison-time in England for
Republican activities.

Jim Gallagher was another friend of my father's who went on
the IRA's bombing campaign in England in 1939. Apparently he
had a job in a factory and one morning when the Special Branch
called there to arrest him for deportation a woman cleaner was
heard to remark "such a nice little man" as Jim was led away.
Jim was indeed genial and loved his pints of Guinness. He was
married to Roseanne Gralton and he worked in the south of Ireland Asphalt Company whose owner, a Mr. Crowley, was very
sympathetic to the IRA. He was the father of Jim Crowley who
played football for Dublin in the 1950s.

Harold Bridges used to call to Cabra Road in the fifties. He
was a very rich businessman who owned a plant-hire firm. He
was non-political but apparently had done some prison time in
England for some offence or other. I think he was from Leitrim
as was his wife Cissie Forde who was a distant cousin of my
father's.

While my father's friends all seemed to enjoy his company,
the wives got on very well too and would spend hours chatting
on Sunday evenings after tea and cakes or brown soda-bread.
My mother's tea making skills were renowned throughout Ireland and her apple tarts and boxtie were a treat to behold. She
was a small sprightly woman and I was very close to her or at
least I wanted to be. I would love getting up early in the morn-

ing so I could be alone with her as she presided over getting the breakfast ready which mainly consisted of porridge, potato cakes or boxtie, a Leitrim dish. The boxtie was delicious and would warm you for the journey down to O'Connells school. We usually went by bus down to Dorset Street and in summer, the buses would have to avoid the cattle driven down the North Circular Road from the nearby cattle-market. This cattle droving continued into the sixties.

In 1952, I joined the altar-boys in St. Peter's Church, Phibsboro and stayed there until 1960. The church with its large steeple is a landmark at the junction between the New Cabra Road and the North Circular Road. I used to serve 7:00 AM Mass and I felt proud, saintly and at peace. I know my mother was proud too and had hopes, I think, that I would become a priest. My brothers too were altar-boys but did not last as long as I did. I remember the Vincentian priests well: Father Cleary, Father McElligott, a bad-tempered person, and a crippled priest, Father Bennett who I would help to get ready at the altar, as he was so handicapped. There was a large fruit-garden at the back of the church with luscious apples and pears and in Summer, we would raid the orchard and sink our teeth into the soft fruit. If you were caught, it meant immediate expulsion, a shame too great to bear. Just as at the convent, there were the May processions with their attendant joys, down the Cabra Road, through the garden and then through the gate on the North Circular Road and back up to the church, banners hard to hold upright if there was a breeze. The procession made me feel important.

At Easter there was a party for the altar-boys and through a misunderstanding, I did not attend one year. The following week, Father Cleary, a robust ruddy man in his sixties, called me aside and gave a box with a cake in it. My mother was delighted. I used to attend Benediction in the evening and can still recall the *Tantum Ergo*. But I could never really manage the thurible, which was too heavy for my small hands. It was a great disappointment to me in later years not to be made head altar-boy on the basis of seniority. When my turn came, Bernard O'Gorman who lived at the end of St. Peter's Road nearby was the one appointed. The issue of seniority was to become a big one for me when I joined the Civil Service in the sixties and, as will be shown later, it had a huge impact on me.

There were two religious Brothers at the Church. Brother Francis, who we called Chinnie because of his jutting chin and Brother Thomas. They were in charge of organising the altar-boys for Mass if a priest needed one in a hurry. Chinnie would enter our room and with his fingers to his mouth and say "Whist!" and we would jump, even if it meant you had to serve a second or third Mass, which I often did. It was a black soutan for ordinary Mass and a red one for a High Mass, which was very solemn. Since St. Peter's was not a parish church, there were never any weddings in my time there. So there were no tips and I never recall getting a tip at a funeral either.

Easter and its exuberance filled me with great joy after the unending Good Friday and the mass of the pre-sanctified on Holy Thursday. Anyway, I always loved the early summer, when hope seemed to abound and the Perpetual Adoration on Ascension Thursday in the evening, when you had to be completely silent for an hour, filled me with a peace that I have not experienced since and doubtless never will. I think then was a period when I was expelled from the altar-boys when Father McElligott caught me and my brother smoking. And during the period of expulsion, I would still get up, pretending to my mother that I was going to serve Mass, as usual. But I was reinstated and continued in St. Peter's until 1960 when I was seventeen and regarded as bit too old to be an altar-boy.

Life rolled on at O'Connells and in third class, I had Mr. Murphy who briefly played football for Kerry, a slick handsome man, but I cannot remember any violence towards the pupils at all. There was one incident, though, like the one in Stanhope Street years earlier. Somebody cut the straps from the schoolbag of another boy and Mr. Murphy threatened us that if the culprit did not own up, we would all be punished. I was terrified and feared that I was going to own up though I was entirely innocent. Eventually a boy owned up and was sent to the Principal for punishment.

In 1954, I made my Confirmation in St. Agatha's Church in North William Street. I wore a grey short-trousered suit and a peaked cap, which had the O'Connells crest and grey socks. The night before I was discussing with my brothers what picture I would go to with my mother for Confirmation day when my father threw a fit and said, "Wouldn't you think you would concentrate on your prayers." My father had no time for the movies and said, "pictures are for those who can't think for themselves," which I always thought absurd. But my father always had these aphorisms in which he believed with great conviction. My mother loved the movies and her favourite stars were Greer Garson and Ronald Coleman. I remember it was a big disappointment to me in the fifties that she did not bring me to see *Random Harvest*, which was being shown in the old Grafton Cinema, which no longer exists. Another film my mother would not bring me to was *Shane*, an epic with Alan Ladd. However, I saw it many times as an adult.

At O'Connells, there was always a chance of a treat on Fridays of a picture in the big hall in the yard styled Janua Coeli Hall, Gates of Heaven. It was, mostly, innocent fare with Laurel and Hardy, Tom Mix and Hoppalong Cassidy. When the film would break down as it often did, we would howl with rage. I think you had to pay six old pence to get in, a tanner it was called then. The film I went to with my mother on my Confirmation day was *The Man in the Grey Flannelled Suit* in the Savoy, which was one huge auditorium at the time.

Despite my father's dictum about films the love of cinema has now gone into the third generation as my children, who are adults, are film buffs and we have many discussions about what is worth seeing. My son, Conor, got me a DVD player for Christmas a few years ago and I have all the TV channels now. As altar-boys, we were always treated to the cinema on St. Stephen's Day in the Bohemian Cinema on Phibsboro Road, which used to be beside the Hut pub. My mother brought us to see *Boystown* with Spencer Tracey and Mickey Rooney in this cinema one Christmas and how we identified with Mickey Rooney, a great actor; he is still to the good.

The old Blackwire Cinema on the North Circular Road across from the library where the Royal Canal used flow was replaced by the State Theatre with great fanfare in the mid fifties. Alas, it is now a carpet store. I had a passionate interest in professional boxing, something I shared with my father in later years. And in 1952, I went to the Blackwire to see the newsreel of the rematch between Sugar Ray Robinson and Randolph Turpin who had beaten the great Sugar Ray in London a few months earlier. I was enthralled as Sugar Ray's victory in New York and remained in the cinema for hours waiting for the rerun of the newsreel, oblivious of what would be said to me when I finally got home.

As I said, the State opened with great fanfare in 1955. I went down that Saturday morning when they were putting the finishing touches on the building and picked up a bit of glass from the rubble as a souvenir. The first pictures shown for the opening were *Where No Vultures Fly* and *West of Zanzibar*, harmless fare for any age as were all the pictures of the era, which could not even offend the sensibilities of my wary father. Suddenly we were let go to the State every Sunday, and we went right up to the sixties where we would meet girls from Eccles Street Convent—Anne Mulligan, Christine Campbell—my very first date, Aideen Muldoon, Geraldine Sweeney whose father had a sweet shop on the Cabra Road and whose mother made desperate efforts to look glamorous. It was in the State that the first budding of youth's dreamy load, as Yeats called it, began to manifest itself. Although my first real kiss did not happen until 1961 when I was nearly eighteen. Indeed, Christine is reputed to have jilted me for Donal Galvin because I was "too slow." The impact those

Sundays at the State had on us as children can be measured by the fact that Rosemarie, my elder sister, cried when she was turned away because the queue was so great. Such innocence seemed beyond her in later years even up to the present day.

In 1954, the new primary school was built in the yard of O'Connells, a two-storey structure with about fifteen class-rooms, all then full to capacity. O'Connells, like many other schools in the city is emptying out now and has a huge quota of foreign nationals; something that pleases me. I think I am now a multicultural pluralist, but who am I to say. There was a grand opening of the new school that night with Mass, as always, dominating the proceedings.

In the summer of 1952, the three boys were sent to Leitrim for holidays. We went with Bill, my father's nephew who lived with us from 1949. Bill's father was Paddy, my father's elder brother who had a tragic life. His wife who was also a Gallogly died when Bill was born and his only daughter, Maureen drowned at the age of sixteen in 1942 in Garadice Lake. Paddy was a railway-man since he was fourteen and had a house, which he built in the twenties but did not move into it until the forties in Ardrum, about two miles from Ballinamore. Paddy got married in the late forties, to Katie Rayle from Dingle—I think it was a match made by the Kellehers across the road from Paddy in Ardrum and Katie made him. She was an ample woman in her fifties when I got to know her first and had been in America for years and her clothes always smelled of mothballs. She was kind, fussy and prim.

Well, Bill left home in 1949 with the intention of going to America but called first to our house in Upper Grangegorman. My father was aghast when Bill told him of his intentions, as my father knew it would devastate Paddy. So my father suggested to Bill that he come and work on the building sites with him and he would teach him the trade and Bill did. Bill was so successful as a carpenter that in 1960 he set up on his own as a builder and now has a thriving business, which he has recently handed over to his son, Padraig. The family are now very wealthy. When my father was in his sixties, he went to work in Bill's workshop who was very kind to him when he was free of hardship on the building sites.

Bill married his childhood sweetheart, Breege Leddy from Belturbet, Co. Cavan in 1952 and I was shattered when I was not asked to the wedding, as I was Bill's godson. Bill and Breege first lived on Kinvara Park, off the Navan Road when they got married and it was Breege who introduced Gerry and me to smoking and Gerry got hooked immediately. Even in those early days in Kinvara Park, Bill and Breege seemed to me to be grandees with style, which we did not have, and I carried a resentment over this for years, mostly on behalf of my mother. But I know now it was all in my head. Bill was always helpful to me lending me money in 1963, when I should have had it myself and bailing me out of trouble later when he negotiated with my father to let me back to the house after he had thrown me out in November of 1963. I still think it was a cruel thing on my father's part to do.

Well the excitement as we boarded the train at Westland Row that summer of 1952 was boundless. The train fare was thirteen shillings and six pence. I think my mother had given us a pound each and I began to worry that I would not have enough after paying the trainfare. But Bill was generous as he gave us all ten shillings—a fortune to a young boy of nine. It was a steam-train and it took hours to get to Dromod where we changed to the narrow-gauge and headed for Ballinamore. I think our first port of call was John Joe McGirl's pub at the bottom of Main Street. The Rowleys and the McGirls were very great as they say in Leitrim, and still are, though John Joe is long dead. I called to see his widow last spring and she is sprightly though now in her eighties. If John Joe suffered for the Republican cause, so did she, when he was in jail.

We stayed in Uncle Jimmy's—my mother's brother and his wife Cassie in their house in Convent Road. Jimmy had a garage across the road from the house and was hard-working and always genial. He was a neat trim man and at 10:00 PM, he would wash himself after work, polish his shoes, and go to John Joe's for a drink with Michael Crossan, who worked in the Convent across the road. I had the pleasure of having a few pints with Michael years afterwards when I went to Ballinamore to make amends for a wrongdoing by me previously. Eddie Matt Turbitt, Cassie's brother, brought us fishing on the canal and this kind, childish man went to the trouble of cutting down the nettles and weeds for us. And before he would cast the line in the canal, he would spit on the wriggling worm "for luck," he would say with a loud guffaw. Eddie was a big handsome man who had the mind of a child and right through my youth, I loved him as a benign uncle. We caught five or six perch that evening and we insisted that Auntie Cassie cook them, though she said, they were all bone. They tasted delicious and I do not think I have ever experienced such joy and happiness as that evening in Ballinamore in 1952. I made friends early and one of my best friends there was Dermot Gannon whose father played football with my father in Drumshanbo in the thirties. Dermot, like his father, became a great footballer and played for St. Mel's, Leitrim and Connacht. I remember he broke my heart in 1960 when he ran riot against O'Connells and scored two goals in the last ten minutes to beat us. We would play football in Tom Roddy's field beside the canal. Tom Roddy had two sons, Tom and Philip who were strong and hardy. Tom senior had a forge down from Uncle Jimmy's garage and I would go in there and watch the sparks fly and hear the bellows roar. Auntie Cassie's family were the Delahydes, and we would visit her Uncle Ned in High Street and he would bellow "Give my regards to Biddy Mulligan, the pride of the Coombe." I would often sleep with Eddie in their big house, the deep innocent sleep of a child and think nothing of it. Nothing untoward ever happened; Eddie Matt was like an innocent child and never married. All that family are dead now but they brought me great joy. Auntie Cassie's father was Hugh

Turbitt who fought in the War of Independence and when he died in 1954, there was a tribute in the Leitrim Observer. He, too, was a blacksmith.

I developed a huge crush on Columba Cryan that year. He was a famous Leitrim footballer and was a wholesale draper. I idolised him. His father, Battie, lived until his nineties and he had a brother, Josie, who was also a footballer. Even though Leitrim was regarded as a weak county football wise, nobody took their football more seriously than the Ballinamore boys did. I saw many a battle in the park down by the railway station. Indeed, I got a huge urge to go to the County final in Carrick-on-Shannon in 1973 and on the spur of the moment took the train down. Allen Gaels versus Ballinamore. It was a great match and Ballinamore won by a flukey goal in the last minute. Naturally, we celebrated in the clubhouse and I got pissed and disgraced myself. Prudence requires that I do not, even now, reveal the details.

When our parents finally came to collect us, something we hated, I cried the whole way home and my father laughed heartily. But I had found a tranquil nirvana in Ballinamore, for I was never happier than in that town right through the fifties. When I go there now to rekindle the memories, it feels to me like a ghost-town, though I met Dermot Gannon there from time to time, who is now in his sixties and looks as fit as a fiddle. Dermot is now a single-handicap golfer and is very droll.

One incident from about 1951 now coming back to me was when we were still in Upper Grangegorman but I had first started at O'Connells. I got off the bus a few stops away from my house to say a prayer in St. Peter's. As I did the Stations of the Cross, my mind began to wander and I insisted with myself that I would continue praying until the wandering stopped. I was, indeed, an unusually sensitive child.

We first started going to Croke Park in the early fifties when my father would bring us and a lifelong interest began to spawn. While we lived within earshot of Dalymount Park and its famous roar, we were never allowed to go there as children as soccer was a foreign game according to my father. Despite this embargo, I would sneak in on my way home from Croke Park and I was there when England played Ireland in the World Cup qualifiers in 1957 when John Atyeo equalised in the last minute, which rendered even Philip Greene of Radio Eireann silent. Croke Park, though, was our first love and we went no matter who was playing every Sunday. Indeed, I still have a photograph of my mother outside Croke Park with some of the children who were too young to go in. My father would stand at the bridge over the canal after the matches hoping to see some of his friends. He did this for many years. We continued to go to Croke Park after my father stopped going with us and have been going ever since. Dublin, my team, was then showing signs of becoming great and won the league in 1953 with nearly all St. Vincent's players. My greatest disappointment as a child was when Dublin were beaten by Kerry in the 1955 All-Ireland final. I was inconsolable which was not helped by Bill's teasing. Dublin were to win the All-Ireland in 1958 with largely the same team.

I have not mentioned Christmas as a child yet. Santa always came to us on Christmas Eve and my father would bring us every year to visit Santa in Clerys. He was demented fending off our wailing queries and he would say "the real Santa is in Clerys." Meanwhile, my mother would be buying the toys and though she would make a shilling go a mile, I can still imagine her keen and frantic eye.

In later years, she would go to John Kelly's shop in Capel Street to buy the toys. John was a famous fiddle player from Co. Clare and a playing companion of my father's. John became famous as did all his children but my father was too modest to project himself. He would prefer to sit by the fire on a Sunday evening, head inclined, eyes closed, entombed in memory *The Sligo Maid*, his favourite and the *Bird in the Bush*. My father modelled himself on Michael Coleman and had most of his records. My father could make a fiddle talk and was self-taught but he could not communicate with his children anyway, though he had numerous friends, as indicated earlier.

On Christmas Eve, my father would reluctantly let us buy fish and chips in the chipper beside us on the Cabra Road. True to form, he could not imagine how anybody would want to spend money, though only sixpence, on what were in fact fried potatoes. But they tasted delicious to us.

While we would be eating our meal in the kitchen, my father would lay out the toys in the sitting-room and set up a contraption to make noise, to indicate Santa's arrival. At a certain point, my father would activate the contraption and we would all dash up the hall, my father first in line and he would pretend to slip on his way and he would swear he saw Santa going up the chimney. One year, he showed us a bit of red flannel, which he said he pulled from Santa's coat. Such elaborate contrivances on the part of my father meant he loved us all in his silent way. But he did not, otherwise, show it. I always was disappointed with what I got, just like my son when he was that age when Santa was believed in.

After tea, Bill and Breege would come down and I would sleep the sound sleep of the just to get up at six o'clock in the morning for High Mass. I was always a sound sleeper as a child and I would kneel at the side of the bed and say my prayers with my brothers. The three of us slept in the one bed and if we play-acted my father would come up to the room and give us a few strokes of his leather strap.

Meanwhile, life continued apace in O'Connells and in fourth class, we had Mr. Galligan whose son was in the class and whose performance, I noticed, had improved considerably under his father's tutelage. I had slipped to thirty-fourth place in the class at that stage. It was Mr. Galligan who prepared us for Confirmation. In fifth class, we had Mr. Moriarty or Micheál Ó Muircheartaigh, as he known on the radio now and he appeared a colossal Adonis with his blonde hair, good looks and tall athletic bearing. He was to do something for me, which I still appreciate.

I had a bad stammer and he called my mother down to the school, which terrified me. But all he wanted to do was to send me to a speech therapist in Clonmel Street, off Harcourt Street. And while my stammer did not go overnight, my speech indeed improved after a weekly session with the therapist. My mother would proudly get me to say a decade of the rosary, which started at 6:30 PM after my father, would come home. He would take off his black beret covered in sawdust and my mother would pour him a bottle of stout and add milk. My father never went to the pub. He just would not waste his hard-earned money on drink or carousing. He was a committed family-man and had values. He was straight and strict, too strict in my view, but would not deal you a lousy card, which I, to my regret, would do in later years.

Mother would pour out a basin of hot water and bathe his feet swollen by the building site. My father was a lumper, as it was called, without a c2 and he never paid tax or insurance. The builders, Jim and John McDonnell would call to the house on Cabra Road with plans for a new housing estate and then my father would price the carpentry end of it. He would give the McDonnells his price, which was usually accepted. And he would draw down £10 a week and get the balance at the end of the contract, which was considerable.

On Saturday morning, my father would turn his back on my mother and take a tenner out of his wallet, always a tenner, and hand it to her in a silent ritual. This went on for years, despite inflation, and my mother in later years would go up to her bedroom and take money out of a bag where my father kept hundreds in notes to supplement her income. He never questioned this practice.

Years afterwards, when we started to work and hand up money to my mother, she would replenish the bag. In the earlier period, my father would give us two shillings pocket money for Croke Park, the pictures or sweets. He was by no means a mean man and would be capable of enormous generosity. If my mother needed money for an outfit for a wedding, he was quite capable of the grand gesture.

My mother did her shopping in Mrs. Flynn's, on Imaal Road just off the Cabra Road, who was a childless widow. She had two sisters, Mary, a spinster who lived nearby and Mrs. Annie Donovan nee Flynn who was married to John Donovan and who had nine children. Mr. Donovan was a Special Branch man and could not abide even constitutional Republicanism a la Fianna Fáil or especially the IRA. He expressed venom for DeValera and how my father was so friendly with him given his IRA intimacies is a mystery to me even to this day. Donovan, as my father called him, went to all the parties in our house when IRA men were present who never felt embarrassed or threatened. My father's IRA friends had no apparent difficulty with his friendship with Donovan who did not generally have a good reputation with Republicans.

The high point of my mother's Christmas was on Little Christmas when she would be invited to a meal with Annie Donovan and her sisters in the Donovan's home in Cabra Drive, off the top of the Cabra Road. Mrs. Bray who lived on the North Circular Road would also come—she was a widow. One year my mother's disappointment was acute when she did not hear word of the annual party in Annie Donovan's. But it was a misunderstanding and word came to her to go up to the house. Her eyes danced with delight as she donned her hat. My mother could easily feel rejected or taken for granted. But these were days of innocence and sometimes joy brought about by simple things you would laugh at today. Simple they were but so much joy would they bring. As a teenager, I would visit the Donovans and Donovan, unrepentant as ever, would pour scorn on the rising star of Charles J. Haughey, a great *bête noire* for him as he was for many years.

One incident from Mr. Moriarty's class springs to mind now. It was the Christmas exam and we were doing the geography test. Mr. Moriarty went out to do a message and I, though knowing the risk, looked up my book *Mountmellick Lace* to be caught in the act by Mr. Moriarty. He put me outside the class but gave me a 40% mark and did not tell my parents. But my parents were dismayed by my results that year as I had slipped to forty-fourth place in the class that Christmas of 1954.

However by summer of 1955, I improved to such a degree that by the skin of my teeth, I got into the scholarship class, which was for one hundred and seventy pounds for second-level education over five years. We had Brother Donnelly and Brother "Killer" Kelly that year and they really put us through the mill, so determined were they that we would succeed in the exam mainly I think to enhance the school's name but I do think as well that they had the boys' welfare at heart. There were brilliant boys in the class. John O'Donoghue, now an eminent doctor and Brian McCarthy, now Secretary to the President, one of the country's top civil servants. Walter Kirwan, John Burke, who became a commandant in the Army and Sean Dalton, who Mr. Moriarty said was the most brilliant boy O'Connells ever had. We all worked like demons but I held up the end of the class by the time the Christmas exams came. All the boys' results were printed on a sheet of paper and the individual boy's name underlined. As an addendum to my report Brother Donnelly wrote, "As regards being the most slovenly and dirty worker in the class, George has no serious rival." My parents did not forgive him for that nor do I even now fifty odd years on. Brother Donnelly was also responsible for another incident involving me later in the school year when he put me out of the class and made me stand out in the corridor nearly all day to look at the bleak walls of Croke Park and the dreary Royal Canal below. He said later that day that none of the boys in the class wanted to have anything to do with me after that. To be rejected by one's peers was a terrible fate especially at twelve. There were a few sadists in O'Connells in my time and Brother Donnelly was one of them. May he rest in peace. The poor man must have had a tortured soul to be so calculating and cruel.

Brother Kelly was not called Killer for nothing but he was fair and not mean. In our spelling tests, you got a biff for every one you got wrong. I remember one test when we were asked to spell *choir*. I began with a *k* but changed it to a *c*. I got belted all the same, as corrections were not allowed for. Brother Kelly hailed from Belfast and eventually left the Brothers and got married. I think I met him and his wife years later. His only son died tragically when he swallowed some tablets that had fallen on the floor of the kitchen. Life is indeed cruel.

Brother Conroy, who was replaced by Brother Kelly in the scholarship class, could not control his violence against the boys at all. I remember that he took John Donoghue's pants down and leathered him. Brother Conroy left the school after that but his was a reign of terror while he was there.

Towards the end of the school year and near the scholarship exam, I was taken out of the class because the Brothers got concerned that I was working too hard. But I returned to do the exam and much to my parents' delight and surprise, I got a scholarship—forty-seventh place in Dublin, which was a major achievement as I was a year younger than most of the boys. My sister, Rosemarie, got one too with one hundred and sixteenth place. However, it caused me great annoyance when my mother then wrote to Auntie Cassie and said Rosemarie had got eleventh in the girls. O'Connells got eighteen scholarships, out of the first twenty that year. When the photograph of the scholarship boys was being taken, I had to borrow a school blazer from another boy for the occasion. It was not that my father could not afford it but he would regard it as a waste of money to buy a blazer just for one occasion, however special that might have been.

Just before the summer, we did the primary State exam, which we all regarded as a laugh after the exertions of the scholarship and I passed it easily. I have no doubt that my parents were very pleased with the double success in the family, though we would have gone to Secondary school, scholarship or no scholarship.

On the social side of things, matters were going well too. In the summer of 1955 just before the scholarship year, Gerry and I went to Ballinamore for our, by now, usual holidays. It was there that my life changed utterly caused no doubt by natural hormonal development. It was the hottest summer in living memory and there have been few hotter since. The fields were parched and Canon Kelly ordered that rain be prayed for at all masses. But the drought continued for weeks on end. I remember Canon Kelly himself coming out to Ardrum where we were staying with Uncle Paddy, with creamery churns but the reservoir too had run dry. And how the tar on the roads melted and we had to get new shoes as the soles of our old ones were ruined and I think I recall Auntie Katie chaffing a little at the cost.

It was that summer of 1955 that I felt the first stirrings of, I would not call it love, but interest in the opposite sex. It was Frances Crossan, who was on holidays from Northampton in England. Her father was a brother of Michael Crossan who I mentioned earlier. Her mother's sister was married to a Mr. Commiskey who owned a sweet-shop beside John Joe McGirl's. The shop is there to this day.

I would go into town early while Gerry would go to Drumrane where Uncle Dan lived who was another brother of my mother's. My mother was born in that house which I am glad to say is now modernised.

I first saw Frances doing cartwheels in her blue dress outside her uncle's shop and knew instantly that boys were different from girls. I was hooked on Frances at once and became quite obsessive about her. She had a brother, Joe, who years later was drowned in Australia and a sister, Carmel. Frances and I would go up to the railway and sit there for hours watching the hissing trains come and go and I would hope to see Uncle Paddy. One day, Frances took me by surprise and said "My mummy says it's a sin to kiss." Kissing was far from my innocent mind but Frances was my girl and all our friends knew we were going together, though I said nothing explicitly to Frances to confirm or deny it. The affair, if it can be called that, lasted while she was in Ballinamore that summer. When it became time to leave in August when my parents came to collect us, I was inconsolable. And Joe Crossan said we would all meet again next year. I was still crying at Kinnegad as the obsession with Frances churned in my soul. I wrote to her a few times and deliberately spelt her name with an *I* in case my mother would come across the letter. Joe sent me a card and said, "Do you still love here?(sic)". Frances did come to Ballinamore the following year but the sparkle had disappeared. I had fried other fish in the meantime, though needless to say, I was sexually immature as I was still only thirteen and knew nothing whatsoever about the facts of life, something my parents never discussed with me. For years, until my late teens, I did not believe sexual intercourse was a conscious act between man and wife. I had even planned to go to England to see Frances at 76, Upper Queen Street, Rushden, Northampton and at school I would look at the atlas and try to pick out Rushden. The family moved to Australia in later years. But I often think of Frances. She was my first obsession, however innocent. She could be a grandmother now, as I am a grandfather. But those lazy tranquil days in Ballinamore down by the canal under the dead heat, catching dragonflies or pinkeens still enchant me. They were the happiest days of my life before adult reality rained its blows on me. But these were savage attacks from within myself, which did me serious psychological damage, which eventually lead to my downfall. Frances and I would walk out to the railway-line and at this point, I can recall one thing we discussed and that was our education. I told her of my hopes to be in the scholarship class come September.

After the scholarship exam and before the summer holidays, we did not have regular classes. But Brother Donnelly introduced us to Latin, which I loved from the outset and quickly mastered. It was to become my best subject in secondary school. Where the gift came from I do not know but I am glad to say, if it is indeed a gift, it has passed on to my daughter, Fionnuala, who is now fluent in Italian and Spanish.

In the 1956 summer holidays, we went to Ballinamore by train and we met Mrs. Mary Reynolds, a Dáil deputy. Her son, Pat Joe Reynolds, later won the seat for Fine Gael, as did, in turn, his son Gerry. Mrs. Reynolds saw my mother weeping as she put us on the train and tried to comfort her. Mrs. Reynolds bought us tea and cakes on the train and we quietly forgot our mother's distress. Though the Reynolds politics were not my father's, we were always friendly with the family. Indeed, I often met Pat Joe when he became a Parliamentary Secretary and see his son Gerry regularly. The family still have a very successful hardware business in Ballinamore and Tess, Pat Joe's widow often serves in the family bar.

I can still see Uncle Paddy, overweight and puffing getting off his bike at Martin's or John Joe's after work for a drink and he had then to cycle the two miles out to Ardrum where he lived but he would have to dismount at the bottom of the Ardrum hill as the incline was too steep. Paddy had a mortal dread of water because of his daughter's death in 1942 and would warn us to avoid the canal. We paid him little attention. I can only remember him getting angry with us once. Gerry and I went into town one morning and told Auntie Katie that we were going to the pictures that night so would not be home until late. The Lyric cinema was up in High Street and was a decrepit building and the films invariably broke down. On that fateful evening in June 1956, Gerry and I went to the pictures oblivious of the concerns of Uncle Paddy who was expecting us home for tea. The film broke down a few times and it was not over until after ten. We went up to Uncle Jimmy's to try to get a lift out to Ardrum. And at his door, who did we see arriving but Uncle Paddy, agitated as hell. We were at the pictures, we blubbered, in our defence but it did not assuage Paddy's anger. Paddy put his bike in the boot of Uncle Jimmy's car and Gerry, in all innocence offered Paddy his seat in the car who cuffed him on the cheek. After that evening, we were banned from going to town much to my distress, as Frances had returned by then. As a response, I threw continuous tantrums and was insolent with Uncle Paddy and Auntie Katie for days, which was uncharacteristic of me.

One night we were allowed to go into town which was the night of the Variety Concert in the local hall and I entered the question time. Much to the embarrassment of my uncles and aunts. I failed to answer any questions for which I got ribbed incessantly afterwards. But I thought I redeemed myself by getting up on stage and singing the complete *Croppy Boy*. Clearly, I had no inhibitions then—these were to come later in life. Precocious Rosemarie won the question-time competition. She had shown signs of a bright future even in her early teens and was then writing poetry for which she won many prizes.

In 1956 too, my interest in Athletics blossomed and my special hero was Ronnie Delaney who first broke four minutes for the mile in June of that year. I remember the excitement at the bus-stop about this and it gladdened by heart as I headed for school.

In June 1956, I would go to the athletics meetings in Landsdowne Road and watch Ronnie race in the mile against Brian Hewson of England. In a photo finish, he was beaten and his performances deteriorated all that summer. He was not expected to be selected on the Irish team for Melbourne; his performances were so poor, let alone win the 1,500 metres gold medal. It was the greatest sporting thrill of my life up to then when he in fact won. I remember the morning well. It was Friday about 8:00 AM and as I got up to hear the broadcast of the race, my mother said, "More in your line to go to Mass." I pretended to go back to bed and as soon as my mother was gone, I went downstairs and turned on the radio, which was up high on a shelf above the kitchen door. Ken Woods, the English miler was first to show, but Delaney kept at the back and I thought his goose was cooked. But then Delaney started to make progress and when he won beating the world-mile record holder, John Landy, into third place, I am still convinced that the English commentator said "I am afraid the Irishman has won." However,

Delaney's foe, Hewson, from earlier in the year came nowhere. To say the least, I was elated. To cap it all that day as well, Floyd Patterson became the youngest person ever to win the World Heavyweight boxing title when he knocked out Archie Moore, an ageing veteran who had held the light-heavyweight title and was a legend.

Thereafter, I placed my boxing dreams and hopes on Floyd Patterson, who in 1960 became the first boxer to regain the world title having been beaten by Ingmar Johannson of Sweden the year before. That was the greatest boxing thrill of my life up to then, though Patterson had a glass jaw, which was proved by the two first-round knockouts by the then awesome Sonny Liston later.

As I said earlier, I shared an interest in boxing with my father and when Patterson was fighting Liston, I called my father about three am Irish time, to get up for the fight. I turned on the radio, which crinkled with static and was hard to hear and as my father entered the kitchen he said "Put on the kettle." Water boiling, tea about to be poured, fight over in the first round. To say we were frustrated would be hardly describing our feelings. Imagine our feelings the following year when there was a re-match. I knock on my father's bedroom door saying "Come on, Dad, the fight is starting." I go down the stairs and put on the kettle and as the kettle was boiling my father came into the kitchen as before, tea poured, fight over. Patterson beaten again in the first round.

That was a few years before the arrival of Cassius Clay to be later known as Mohammed Ali. Being a contemporary of mine, I thought Ali was the greatest ever and many fans did too, but my father averred Joe Louis held the accolade as the greatest. But my father was always captivated by Ali's antics. When Ali beat Liston in 1964, I was shamelessly over the moon but my father would reiterate that Louis was the greatest. It is impossible to prove but the arguments always bring heated debate especially in the pub. And the argument of who was the greatest of all time will, I hope, go on forever.

In the spring of 1956, we first ventured out to the lane at the back of our house, which also ran at the back of the corporation houses at Newgrange Road, and quickly made friends. My father did not approve of our playing with children from corporation houses; however, we got our way and played out the back for years. My father had built two garages at the end of our garden, which had access to the lane. He used one of them for his own car and rented out the other, first of all, to a motorbike mechanic, Paddy, who soon got behind in his rent, much to my father's annoyance. Across the lane from our house lived the Harlings who had a sweet factory and next were the Kennys and the Doyles. Mr. Doyle was a pavement foreman with Dublin Corporation and had four girls who were very friendly with my sisters. Mrs. Doyle died when the children were not quite teenagers. The Doyles always went on continental holidays, a source of great envy for me. Mr. Doyle's brother, Kevin, lived with them; he was a bachelor and his main past-time was playing snooker. As an adult, I often watched Kevin playing snooker in a hall in O'Connell Street. Mr. Gleeson lived next to the Doyles; he was a civil servant in the Department of Lands and I often met him on my way to lunch when I, too, joined the civil service. Mrs. Gleeson was ill a lot of the time and there were at least two sons, one of whom, Paddy, became a priest. The Reids lived further down the lane and one of the daughters, Breda, won many All-Ireland medals playing camogie for Dublin. We always called Mrs. Reid "Fattser", but naturally not to her face. The Williams's lived next to the Reids and we were friendly with the boys. Down at the bottom of the lane where we would play soccer, lived the Reillys. This was a large family and we were very friendly with Paddy and his sister, Alice. The railway, which passed at the bottom of the lane, ran from the nearby Broadstone and was in use up to the late fifties at least.

When my father would arrive at his garage on a winter's evening, he would go mad if he caught courting couples in the headlights of his car. Sex was never talked about or even acknowledged at that time or even later. Sometime early in the summer of 1956, I got friendly with Eileen Farrell and Terry Sheedy from Dowth Avenue who used to come to our lane to play. I was soon "going with" Eileen, though like with Frances nothing was said but everybody knew we were going together. Though, in fact, we never went anywhere, for example going to the pictures or anything else. We just played in the lane in that unending summer and would not go in until nightfall. At some point later in the summer, Eileen broke "it" off and I was a little distressed. The mood soon evaporated when we headed for Leitrim in August.

At the bottom of the lane we would have battles royal, playing soccer, much to the annoyance of an old man who lived there. I cannot recall his name now. No quarter was asked for or given in these games. "We'll play up to twenty," we would say; then it became thirty and so on until darkness fell. Anto and Ray Tormey, who also lived in Newgrange, were the first teddy-boys I ever saw and when they went to England, how I envied them. Ray definitely had heavy-soled blue suede shoes and the DA haircut. He was the real thing, I thought. When I got older, I became aware of card-schools on a Sunday morning at the bottom of the lane when large sums, to me anyway, were won and lost. We would watch in childish awe, as the pots got bigger and bigger. We continued playing in the lane until our late teens at least.

In September 1956, on the basis of my scholarship results and the fact that I was a year younger than the rest of the class, I entered 1A class. Most of the boys who did better than me in the scholarship and were older went into 2A. I was really happy in that class with the affable Brother Tracey as Principal teacher with Mr. Ryan as assistant. Mr. Ryan had a glass eye and we unkindly called him "Popeye" while we nicknamed Brother Tracey "Dick". That was an easy year study-wise, as there was no public exam, only Christmas and Summer in-house tests in which I was to do very well.

Brother Tracey would always pull an apple or an orange from his cassock and reward a boy if he answered a question correctly. He would also put certain boys sitting on his lap, though there were no sexual implications in this. Brother Tracey was straight-up and was just being kind; he loved children and had no hesitation in showing it. I would like to put it on record that I never experienced or witnessed any sexual abuse in O'Connell's in my eleven years there. Physical and emotional abuse were routine but I never came across anything of a sexual nature in my time there. When we became sexually aware, there were some rumours about some of the brothers. So innocent was I of ordinary sexual matters, I could never conceive of sexual abuse of young boys at the school or anywhere else. One of the great pleasures of Brother Tracey's class was the reading of *Treasure Island* and he would get the boys to read out the different parts. Like Brother Mullane's class years earlier, I enjoyed the pleasure of reading, and loved the escapism of *Treasure Island*, with Billy Bones, Captain Smollet, Jim the hero and, of course, Long John Silver who would be hard to forget as a boy.

The year passed unknown to us into 1957, when the Russians launched the first Sputnik into space. We would scan the sky at night to see if we could catch a glimpse of the Sputnik and to our delight often did. I was later in 1961 to see Yuri Gagarin, the first astronaut in space, in London after I was working in the pea factories in Norfolk. It was the summer holidays of 1957 that I got my first job, in Mr. O'Shea's, a Kerryman, in Little Denmark Street off the bottom of Parnell Street. O'Shea was a joiner who assembled tables and chairs and my job, and Jesus was it tedious, was to sand the wood to get it ready for varnishing. When this was done, Mr. O'Shea would varnish the wood and when dry, assemble it for delivery to Arnotts or Roches Stores. My wages were a pound a week and I gave 17/6 of that to my mother, which she expected anyway. I kept the remaining 2/6 for the pictures—you could get in for sixpence and sweets. The work was a grind and I got to hate it with a vengeance but I stuck it out until August when we went to Ballinamore for our annual holidays. But the old sparkle had evaporated by then. In that summer, Evelyn Bond who lived in the prison cottages on the North Circular Road developed a crush on me and we arranged to go to the State one Saturday afternoon but I funked it, making a feeble excuse. Anyway, I was more interested in Imelda Flanagan who lived in Goldsmith Street off the North Circular Road but this really came to nothing.

In my last week working, I asked Mr. O'Shea for a rise and he said he would give me a 2/6 rise the following week. I blurted out, "I'm leaving next week," and he gave me the rise, chaffing a little. I went to see the film *Twelve Angry Men* in the State the day I left the job. It was a great film and still is.

We headed off to Ballinamore the following day and stayed, as usual, in Uncle Paddy's and Auntie Katie's. The first time I ever had cornflakes was in that house. We rarely went to Kiltubrid, near Drumshanbo where my father was born; the house is still there and indeed my son has recently bought it with a view to its being a holiday home for him and his family. But the house in the fifties was a long since empty as all the family of seven had emigrated to the States in the twenties except my father and Uncle Paddy. I always felt it sad that my grandparents lost most of their children through emigration especially as communication was so difficult. There were four girls in that family, all very musical and all beautiful singers like my father. When I went to the States in 1982, I met all the sisters. Uncle Barney was dead by then. He was my father's other brother. He was a die-hard republican and fought in the War of Independence and I think the Civil War. He is reputed to have been on the run and escaped to America and was fond of drink. Gerry still has his revolver. My father was haunted by his memory. Barney got married, reluctantly, it was said when he was in his forties but my father never saw him again. A photograph of him shows him to be old with a bitter look. When I was leaving the States in 1982, I met my father at Kennedy Airport where he and my brother Gerry were arriving. It was an emotional encounter. My father had a ball with his sisters and their children with many parties thrown in his honour. He died the following year but more about that later.

I very seldom went to Drumrane, where my mother was born. Uncle Dan, her brother, was a hard-working farmer on the land he had inherited from his father, James. He struck me as humourless but that was through the eyes of a child. He was to die of a heart-attack at a match in Ballinamore in 1962, aged fifty-seven. Uncle Jimmy died aged forty-nine, also from a heart attack in 1964. They were unfortunate to have lived at the wrong time. Had it been forty years later their premature deaths would have been avoidable with modern day bypasses and so on. In fairness to Uncle Dan, how could he have humour, with a family of six to feed on the same small holding his father left him.

My mother had three sisters abroad. Aunt Katie and Aunt Anne in the States and Aunt Molly, a nurse in England who had married a brother of Auntie Cassie who was married to Uncle Jimmy. Auntie Molly died in a road accident in January 1962 when she was cycling home from work. She was in her early forties. It was considered a good idea after her death to bring her two youngest sons, John and Kevin, to be raised by Uncle Jimmy and Auntie Cassie in Ballinamore. Uncle Jimmy's and Aunt Cassie's joy was short-lived for Uncle Jimmy died in August 1964. So John and Kevin went back to England to be raised by their father, Hughie Turbitt. When Auntie Cassie died some years ago, she left her two houses, one each to Kevin and John, who now live in Ballinamore. I met Kevin recently in Smith's Bar in the town where he works.

Auntie Katie in the States married Billy Garry, a gentleman by all accounts, but Billy died when their two children, Billy and Mary Anne were young.

I met Auntie Katie in the States when I went there in 1982 and I nearly died of shock—she was the dead spit of my mother. Aunt Anne, known as Cissy, married Johnny Brodisan and they had one son, Johnny, but this marriage by all accounts was not a happy one. Auntie Katie and Auntie Anne came to visit us in 1964 with Katie's daughter, Mary Anne. I remember well, Uncle Jimmy sobbing as we left his two sisters to the airport. He was dead within a week of that. Happiness is indeed transient.

I always call to visit Drumrane, my mother's birthplace, when I go to Ballinamore and unfailingly get a warm welcome from my cousin Vincie and his wife Anna McGovern who is kindness itself. No problem for her to throw up a big feed and drive me back to town afterwards to my hotel. Anna was a secretary to John Joe McGirl and I think that is where Vincie got his Sinn Féin leanings from, though there was no politics that I know of in the Gallogly family, not Republicanism anyway. I think they were Fine Gaelers. Anna left John Joe's when his son Liam started running the pub and got married. Two women under the one roof never pull together. Anna would have typed up John Joe's speeches and done all his office work. In addition to being a publican, John Joe was an undertaker, a bicycle mechanic and an auctioneer.

So within the space of two years or so, half the Gallogly family were wiped out. It was Bill who brought the bad news on each occasion to my mother who was devastated by her losses. The only time she was ever out of Ireland was when she went to England for Auntie Molly's funeral. She was always after my father to bring her to America to see her sisters but he would not go, and when he finally went in 1982, it was too late. My mother was dead after a long battle with cancer, which crippled her until she died in 1977, to leave my father a broken man, never to recover, with attendant regrets. But regrets are futile and my father would shake his head and mournfully say, "What will I do now?"

In 1957, I got my first dog—Lucky; he was a tanned and white fox-terrier and he would sleep in the garage. Lucky filled my cup of joy to the brim and I would bring him for walks to the nearby Phoenix Park and let him swim in the dog pond. I only had him for a year when he died of distemper. Before he died, he would get very angry and would snap at me if I went to pat him on the head. He died in early July 1958 and I was heartbroken. The children had a funeral "service" for him much to my father's amusement, though he helped to dig the grave. We put a cross on his grave, which my father thought was ridiculous. My grief only lasted for a few days because of the fact that the Yankees arrived home—my father's two sisters, Molly and Nora and Nora's husband Jim Lynch and their daughter, Leonora; Auntie Molly's daughter Sue also came but more of that later and back to 1957.

Tommy Gallagher was in Brother Tracey's class with me at that time, was always messing, and would pick on me especially. I complained to my mother and she promptly came down to the school to meet Brother Tracey in an effort to get Tommy to leave me alone. I only got to know about it a few days later when I was rolling a marble on my desk and Brother Tracey upbraided me. He told the class scornfully, "This is the boy who complained to his mother about Tommy Gallagher messing with him now he is messing himself." But the incident had little affect on me. Tommy and I became great pals. He was a great character and lived at the junction of Jones' Road and Clonliffe Road. I have not seen him since I left school in 1962.

One evening in about May 1957, I was down at the end of the backlane playing and for no reason I scaled the barbed-wire railings at the bottom, crossed the railway, and climbed the embankment into Cabra Park. Now the houses in Cabra Park were really posh, at least to my then childish mind. I then met new friends, Geraldine McVeigh whose father was a doctor and whose son Paul became my father's doctor when he was in his seventies. There was Paula O'Rourke with her red chubby face, the Becketts, Bobby and Renee and the standoffish Mary Rose Greville. I soon was part of this gang and spent many a long summer's day and evening playing with them. I was even invited to a party in the McVeighs as I was now going with Geraldine.

Now this posed problems because of my father but, somehow, I got going and had a great time dancing to the latest Rock and Roll records. Ita, Geraldine's elder sister was a great bopper but I was shy and awkward.

One evening, there was a knock on our door and who was there but Geraldine and Paula looking very chic in bobby-socks and the latest fashion. I nearly died with mortification and the incident was the subject of amused comments by my family for some time afterwards. One Saturday morning, when I was still in Brother Tracey's class, I bought Geraldine a ring; it was only a cheap one and gave it to her. She was delighted. But the relationship, such as it was, petered out, entirely platonic I can tell you. Mr. McVeigh continued to have a paternal interest in me and in the early sixties, I would meet him in the Hut and he would enquire how I was doing in the Civil Service and advised me to study at night. He was an enlightened and kind man. I have not seen or heard of Geraldine since the late fifties, and there are no more surprising knocks on my door.

I first became aware of the burgeoning craze of rock and roll in 1954 when Frank O'Hare who was in my class, stopped outside a record shop in Phibsboro and pointed out a picture of Elvis Presley on the dust-sheet of an LP and I was immediately captivated. Frank, I learned recently, is now dead. Late in about 1956, I think, on Sunday evenings, we would turn on Radio Luxembourg, after my parents went out on a visit. The first tune I recall was *Sixteen Tons* by Tennessee Ernie Ford and the beat did something for me that night that has stayed with me up to the present day. Though I did not start to go to the tennis club hops until 1959, I learned all the pop songs of the day by heart. I remember well Doris Day's *Que Sera* with its catchy melody on the radio one Saturday morning in 1956.

In fact, my first public performance took place in 1956 in the Father Matthew Hall in Church Street when I entered a talent contest and sang an Elvis song, *All Shook Up*, and shared first prize—it did not matter to me that there were only two entries.

My father's response was, "Wouldn't you think you'd sing an Irish song?" It was not until the sixties that I came out of my father's shadow and embraced traditional Irish music and I, in fact, became a fairly good exponent of Irish ballads in English, something I do even to this day.

But rock and roll was my first love and I later became proud to possess an LP of Elvis' Greatest hits which I continued playing into the seventies when my children were young. I do not want you to think I am always knocking my father but I need to record the influences, which had such a bearing on my later life. One day I was playing an Elvis record over and over on the old radiogram, which my father had made, in the dining room when my father got so annoyed with it that he smashed it into pieces. This actually occurred. All that I have written so far happened and I am doing my best to record it truthfully, though my memory may be a little flawed but that is not a deliberate thing just to show my father in a bad light.

In September 1957, we went into second year and had Brother Keyes as principal teacher, a very nervous man who was ill-equipped to teach boys of the modern era. We had Bob Kavanagh who dressed nattily, who taught us English and Noddy Kavanagh for Science. We literally drove Brother Keyes mad, as he could not hack it at all. He put me in charge of collecting the water pistols from the boys and locking them in the press, when confiscated. But I would sell the pistols back to the boys and when Brother Keyes found out, he averred, "I am afraid, George, you are not to be trusted anymore." He only lasted a few months and was reputed to have left to teach in England, not before our reputation for indiscipline had gone around the school. Bob Kavanagh was a gambler and he would often slip-out of the class to bet even when exams were being held. He was very precise and immaculately turned out but he had a mean, venomous streak in him. He enjoyed a huge reputation in and outside the school as a teacher of English and many of his students went on to win scholarships.

Noddy Kavanagh, we nearly drove mad as well and he could not control us in the Science Lab at all—he was new to the school. One day he had a trainee from Africa under his tutelage and we were boiling water under pressure. We pretended that the rubber hose was fully sealed, though it was not, and the water boiled vigorously threatening to explode. Noddy and his African student nearly had a fit and we were reported to Brother Laffan, known as Ghandi, the iconic teacher of Science who we were to have the following year for Inter Cert. Our reputation for trouble further increased when we had Ghandi the following year; he never stopped berating us for our mischievous antics in second year. Under Brother Keyes, second year was a doss but then Brother Rocket came to knock us into shape and begod he did. He was a pocket-sized bull of a man and he dished out punishment left, right and centre.

The 1957/58 school year ended almost unknown to us, as it was soon summer holiday time again. We got our holidays at the end of May and I got a job in Hugh Jordan & Co., bar-fitters in St. Mark's Lane beside Westland Row; the wages were much better than the previous year and I got 37/6 a week of which I gave my mother 30/-.

*Bondage in a summer job brought maturity with thirty bob...*Three brothers ran the business, Hugh, Christy and Paddy Jordan and I was working in the stores at the back where we would pack glasses in straw and put them in boxes for dispatch to all parts of the country. It was easy work but it was not helped by the fact that the Jordans were bullies and conducted a reign of terror. Christy, known as "Mr. C" was in charge of the factory and stores and his rule was law. We would only see Hugh occasionally but when we did, you would shiver, I can tell you. Paddy was the nicest. You would only meet him towards the weekend when he would come with his orders following his travels in the country. Aidan Donoghue who was in my class warned me about taking a job at Jordan's as his brother had worked there the previous year but I had to find out things for myself. I was transferred to the factory for a period and the work was murderous under the supervision of a bullying foreman. I had to fill the hoppers with crown-corks and climb steps to do so with a basket full of them on my shoulders. I was not strong and was quite unused to physical work of any kind and the foreman would sneer at my efforts. Another job I had had in the factory was waxing the tin-plate before it was converted by machines into crown-corks. Having been fed into the hoppers, the crown-corks would be ready for the cork disks. My time in the factory did not last long and I was soon back in the stores. Paddy was the foreman there and he was a gentleman. His wages would have been about £5 per week, not quite a princely sum. There was also a cynical weather-beaten man in his fifties, named Tom, who gave me a lot of advice in relation to bosses whom he could not abide. He used say, "Never admit to anything."

The horse and cart driven by a Paddy for CIE would collect the boxes of glasses to bring them to the railway station for dispatch to the country. I always prayed that the fragile contents would arrive in one piece. Hugh Jordan and Christy kept a sharp eye out for breakages. One Saturday morning, the boys in the stores at the back were getting rid of broken glasses and I was on look-out up the front pretending to be sweeping but Hugh Jordan came out and rushed down the factory to the stores and I thought we were all goosed. However, Paddy the foreman had had a lookout from a hole in the wall of the stores and the day was saved. We finished at one on Saturday morning and at about twelve thirty, I was reading the paper, as I had finished my work but who would come into the stores but Christy and he said, "You're sacked." I turned on my heel to leave and he said "I was only joking. Have you no sense of humour?" So I came back. The Jordans had trouble holding on to staff. St. Mark's Flats were next to the factory and Hugh and Christy would try to get the women there to come and work for them on the crown-cork machine. These women were a cheerful bunch and I was in awe of their accents. I was to work in Jordan's the following year as well. One June evening, I was rostered for some overtime and while I would normally jump at the chance of making extra money, I was reluctant this time. There was an athletics meeting that evening in Santry Stadium with the irrepressible Billy Morton in charge of proceedings. So I badly wanted to go and I got out of the overtime. This was the night Herb Elliot of Australia broke the world record for the mile in a time of 3:54:5 and the first five were under four minutes—and our own Ronnie Delaney getting third behind Marvin Lincoln also from Australia, to the jeers of some of the crowd. His Olympic success was now just a memory with these boors. Four world records were broken in that month in 1958, one mile, two miles, three miles and four miles. It was a great thrill for me, a boy not yet fifteen, to witness these heroics.

Two other things of significance happened that month which I flagged earlier. My dog Lucky died and two days later, the Yanks arrived. I saw the green Ford Consul pull up outside our gate, and rushed in to tell my parents. There were tears and joy all round, as my father had not seen his sisters since 1931. My mother surpassed herself with the feast she put on and my parents would not hear of it when the Yanks said they would stay in a hotel. Somehow, sleeping quarters were found for them all including Louise Thomas, a friend of Aunt Mollie's and she would say, "Call me Aunt Louise." This I frankly and vehemently refused to do. Bill and Breege arrived and the hooley lasted well into the night—the drink was flowing too. My parents were ideal hosts. Jim Lynch, Aunt Nora's husband had brought hundreds of cartons of Kent cigarettes, which he got duty-free and later on, Gerry and I would raid his case from under his bed, and sell on the cigarettes to our friends at knock-down prices. That was when my father sang and played. My two cousins Leonora and Sue were beautiful singers too, as were Aunt Mollie and Aunt Nora. My mother had not a note in her head but her party-piece was *Off to Dublin in the Green* which she would sing with great gaiety after two gin and tonics—then doing the Hokey

Pokey kicking her legs in the air with great heart and gusto. But my father was the darling of them all with his old Irish ballads and his own compositions. They never tired of him and he would pick a tune from a stone. He had such an ear for music, all self-taught. Where we all slept, I do not know but it was a happy house that night and we would recall that night in July 1958 with great nostalgia when I, for one, saw my parents in a different light and had a feeling of great pride. I cycled off to work in Jordan's the following morning in high do, bringing with me some cartons of Kent cigarettes for sale. I had huge guilt about this afterwards and was afraid to confess it in confession. I was still an altar-boy and would feel compelled to receive communion during Mass, though I might not have been to confession. I was beginning to feel the painful fear of going to confession and the palpable relief afterwards. I was beginning to have impure thoughts then but did not act on them but they bothered me; I was an innocent abroad as regards sex and had never experienced the mildest form of sex at that point in my life.

I remember once going to confession to a Father Lyons and confessing that I had deliberately gone to see an obscene film. He was surprised that there could be such a thing because of the strict censorship laws in Ireland then. All it was, was women in bikinis in the circus but even this aroused me. Fr. Lyons was very understanding when I blurted out my guilt, as I saw it, and only gave me a light penance. My relief knew no bounds as I left the church.

The Yanks stayed for a month and we had a big party one Saturday for them. All my father's friends were to be invited and it was my job to cycle all around the city to tell them. I had got a bike the previous Christmas and because it was second-hand, I was disappointed. My father even got a firkin of Guinness for the occasion and the food, all prepared by my mother, was fit for kings. My father was in his element and he played all his tunes and sang his songs. Aunt Mollie sang the *Shawl of Galway Grey*, a ballad I have been meaning to get for years now. Aunt Mollie was an established composer of some renown in the States. She was married to Tal Eager from Kerry, whom I met when I went to the States in 1982. I think he worked in the Post Office. All that generation is dead now and I am glad we did not look to the future that glorious night in August 1958. Paddy Earley was in charge of the drink and as he was not much of a drinker himself, he kept a sharp eye on everybody especially those who were fonder of it than he was. Jim Lynch was partial to a drop of whiskey and smoked cigarette after cigarette non-stop. He hailed from Granard, Co. Longford and there are some of the Lynchs still there. He died in 1960 just before Aunt Nora was to make another trip home. She was devastated by her loss and when she came home, again she would spend a lot of time in bed reading spiritual books. Nothing could surpass the golden 1958. I remember Hughie McCormac reciting *The Old Fenian Gun* with all the actions. Hughie was a great entertainer and I would go to hear him mainly for recitations in O'Donoghues when the ballad-craze began in the 1960s. His *Races at Punchestown* was marvellous and I am sorry I did not learn it from him when I had the chance. Though my father taught Hughie the fiddle, he was not great at it but he played with great heart. His wife was a patient in the Gorman for years, on and off, and he would visit her on Sundays on his motorbike. Hughie liked the crack and I loved him playing the *Battering Ram*, a reel he would play with abandon. Mr. Donovan did not need much persuasion to sing his party-piece, a ballad called *The Donovans*, completely at home amongst all the IRA men. The party lasted until dawn and we all went to Mass in St. Peter's Church at 7:00 AM exhausted but happy. Incidentally, Hughie served time in the Curragh during the war and was taught Irish by Martin O'Cadhain there. He had two brothers, Bertie who owned a few grocery shops on the southside and another brother who made a fortune by selling his land in Meath for mining.

Though my interest in Leitrim had waned by 1958, I cried and cried when my mother told me that we were not going that year because of the Yanks' visit. I remember lying on the bed in the "maid's room" crying bitterly for hours. However, I went for one day with Bill, Jim Lynch and Leonora but it was no good to me. That evening on the bog-lane on the way to Drumrane, Leonora tried to kiss me in a friendly gesture but even though I had a bit of a crush on her—she was beautiful at twenty-four, I recoiled with boyish embarrassment. On the way home Uncle Jim stopped the car in Kinnegad to go to the toilet saying "I gotta see a man about a dog," which I took literally and questioned him repeatedly about the dog afterwards. My father was heartbroken the evening the Yanks left for home and got into a foul humour after they had gone. "Things will be different from this day on," he said ominously. But there were no immediate repercussions that I can recall.

Then back to school in September 1958 when Dublin won the All-Ireland. Joe my elder brother was photographed with Kevin Heffernan, the captain, holding the Sam Maguire aloft and the picture appeared in all the papers, which delighted the family. That school year was the Inter Cert year and we had Brother Curtin as principal teacher who taught us Irish and Maths. He was very accurately nicknamed the Bull by his appearance matched only by his barbarism to the class. He had a notorious reputation for corporal punishment—too benign a term. To offset that, we had Mr. Sheehan for Latin and I was to become his pet as I excelled at the subject. Like most of the teachers in O'Connells, Mr. Sheehan had a system for getting the best results. The teachers knew the curriculum by heart and adapted their teaching notes to what they anticipated would invariably wind up in the exam. I soon was to outshine the other boys in Latin but one of the reasons was that I studied very hard in that year often five or six hours a night, nearly up to eleven o'clock, when my mother would insist I would go to bed. I felt I had no choice but to study like a demon, as my father would always remind us all of the hardship on the building sites, which had to be avoided at all costs. One day, he brought home a big slice of dry brown bread and showed it to us as if this proved everything. "This is what my apprentice had for his lunch today," he said, waving the crust in the air. It struck home to me anyway, though Gerry laughed through it all preferring to read comics than to study.

My brother Joe studied hard too but I think he had more natural ability than I had. He was to get an Intermediate scholarship and University scholarship and was awarded the best boy of the year prize on leaving school in 1960. Two years after that, I was expelled. But I had to swot harder than most and swot is what I did. I could master any subject by the sheer force of swotting, something that was sneered at by some of the boys. The boys most admired were those who had obvious ability but did not study—real anti-heroes, I suppose. To this day, I do not know how bright or otherwise I was but my lack of confidence in my abilities was to cause me untold difficulty in later years.

In 1959, the Inter Cert year, we had Mr. O'Sullivan for History and like the rest of the teachers, he had a system and had this down to a fine art and his results proved it. He had well prepared notes, *as Gaeilge*, and our hands would fall off us taking them down. Mr. O'Sullivan was from Co. Kerry and I got friendly with his nephew, Micheal when I was an adult. Mr. O'Sullivan was very well-groomed but not as trendy as Bob Kavanagh from second year was. But unlike Bob Kavanagh, who was conscious of his own vanity, Mr. O'Sullivan was very self-effacing despite his reputation. I see him now with his finely creased blue suit and highly polished brown shoes reading the History notes to us without a break until the class ended. I still recall his pleasant smile. We did European and Irish history and I still have the notebooks to this day.

Brother Curtin was not a good teacher—we had him for Maths and Irish and his bullying behaviour was outrageous. He gave Tommy Gallagher an awful time. But Tommy was obstinate and obdurate and the more punishment he got the more he provoked the Bull into giving him more. I sat beside Tommy Lyons, the school's best footballer who later became a soccer international as an amateur. Brother Curtin could not tolerate soccer but he made an exception in the case of Tommy Lyons. The Bull implied one day that I was copying off Tommy Lyons and did not realise that it was the other way around until later in the year. Brother Curtin did not have a system and seemed to have no teaching ability at all. I have no doubt that I would have got an Intermediate scholarship in 1959 if I had a better teacher. But the Bull was capable of kindness too—on the morning of the Geometry exam he came up to me and gave me a geometry set and I am sure that this was the real Brother Curtin. It was just that he was unsuitable for teaching and his violence was caused by, I think, frustration on account of this. Shortly after the Inter, Br. Curtin and Br. O'Connor who taught Gerry started to come to our house for a social evening and they would have their bottles of stout or whiskey and would enjoy themselves immensely. Brother Curtin was the trainer of the football teams and one of the high points in 1959 was the school winning the Leinster Junior Championship with Jim "Pop" Clinton as the inspirational captain. I will give more details later.

In the Inter Cert year in 1959, we had Brother Laffan, nicknamed Ghandi, after the Indian pacifist, as he resembled him so much, gaunt in the extreme. He came to O'Connells about the time of Ghandi's assassination. Brother Laffan taught us Science and he was a genius at it but his genius did not rest easily with him as he had a violent temper and a vicious sarcastic tongue. If the Bull's tactics were sheer brute-force, Ghandi's were to instil terror—you could feel the atmosphere in the Science room. They must have been tortured souls, these poor men that they were so brutal in their treatment of young boys. You could never relax in Ghandi's class—when you least expected it—Ghandi would hiss "Clean sheet, boys"; that meant a test to see if we had done our homework the night before. I was, in a way, at a disadvantage as my brother Joe was excellent at Science and Ghandi was always making comparisons, much to my discomfort—though I was to do well in the subject for two years, I did the Inter in 1959 and

1960. Ghandi was up-to-date with all the developments in Science though he was now in his sixties and showed no signs of waning. When we would be outside the Science class waiting to go in, we would ask the boys coming out, "What's he like?" and they would throw their eyes up to heaven. So great was the fear in our hearts, you could feel the intimidating atmosphere as you sat down, not knowing when the "Clean sheet" would be proclaimed but came it always did. But I enjoyed the experiments in the laboratory, and soon I was to get my own chemistry set which later became a marvel to me—I especially remember the smell of the noxious gasses and the wonder of the bubbling acids. We loved it when Ghandi would generate Hydrogen Sulphide, with its fart-like smell and we would howl with laughter—the joke being lost on Ghandi. Most boys in the class stole stuff from the laboratory, to bring home and Ghandi copped on. He once caught a boy stealing mercury and I can still hear his sarcastic sneer. "It fell into his pocket," he said. Ghandi was from Kilkenny and had a whining voice. For all his faults he was a great teacher and the results we all got proved it. He was very proud of my brother, Joe, who went on to do Science at University and held him up as an example to all, especially me, I thought.

I prepared well for the Inter Cert in 1959, studying like a demon and my efforts bore fruit in abundance. I got over ninety per cent in Latin and Science and got full marks in History, a feat that was repeated by two other boys, Jimmy White and Peadar Ward. But I only got 70% in Maths and Irish, which meant that I did not get a scholarship. Still, I was pleased, my parents too, but what most of all, the Brothers were also pleased. One of them said, "Are you trying to outdo your brother Joe?" The exam did not start off well though, in my head anyway. When we did the Arithmetic exam the first morning, the Bull arranged for some boys in other classes to do the sums while we were sitting the exam. When we were finished, we were made compare our efforts to the correct answers. As far as I was concerned, I got none of the sums right and this did my head in. This seeming failure was on my mind when we went to do the next exam but my results in Arithmetic proved how wrong I was as I got 175 out of 200 in the exam. But it shows you what kind of tricks my mind began to play on me—a thing that was to have more serious implications for me when I got older. On the basis of my results and the fact that I was a year younger than most boys doing the Inter, the head Brother, Brother O'Connell suggested to me—and a suggestion by Brother O'Connell was to my mind an imperative—that I would have a very good chance of a scholarship if I repeated the Inter in 1960. My mother was reluctant but I convinced her that the brothers were right, so I entered 4A the scholarship class in September 1959. Brother Muldowney was my principal teacher and he taught us English and Maths. He was a genius and he was sensitive and gentle with a great sense of ironic humour. He was musical and an artist and painted all the scenes for the annual school opera. In short, he was a joy. We had Mr. O'Sullivan from the year before for History and Irish, Mr. Sheehan again for Latin and Brother Laffan for Science, all great and talented teachers and who brought out the best in the boys. Mr. O'Sullivan approached Irish as he did History reading out his well-researched notes for us to copy which we did, word for word. I continued to shine at Latin and remained Mr. Sheehan's pet, my results in the previous Inter Cert justifying his faith in me. Terror, though, still reigned in the Science room.

In about April of 1960, tragedy struck the class next door 3A—a boy not more than fifteen hanged himself in a pure accident when he was playing Cowboys and Indians on the high window-ledge. The whole school was stricken with shock and Brother Muldowney blamed himself for leaving the boys unsupervised at lunch-hour and, of course, the papers made hay of it to accentuate Brother Muldowney's distress. Paul Harte was the boy's name and his parents never got over his death. Nor did Brother Muldowney. He left O'Connells after the Inter, was believed to have taken to drink, and tablets which killed him prematurely. He finished his teaching days in Tuam Christian

Brothers School. What a talent.

In May 1959, the big match between O'Connells and St. Finian's, Mullingar was played in Navan and we filled the train on its way to the town singing "OC, OC, OCS will we win Yes, Yes, Yes." Well as I said earlier, we won with Pop Clinton playing a blinder. Pop, who was later to become a Garda, was from the north county as was Paddy Fagan who played at midfield. But it was Tommy Lyons and Denis Ward in the forwards whom I looked up to most. I always think forwards have the more glamorous role in football. I have never experienced such elation as when we won—and we triumphantly marched up Talbot Street from the train station singing to the air of *Old Lang Syne* "We're here because, we're here because, we're here because we're here," repeated over and over.

I worked again in Jordan's the summer of 1959 and went to Leitrim in August for my holidays where I met a host of new friends. Liam and Padraig Wynne, Matt McCartin, and of course girls, Kitty Holland, Hilary Gannon, Dermot's sister, Mary Duignan, Mary McGirl, John Joe's niece and Mary Logan, the butcher's daughter who was to write to me a lot later to my acute embarrassment. The weather was glorious and I would go fishing with my cousins in Drumrane, crossing the metal bridge over the canal, having walked down the railway keeping a sharp lookout for trains. One night I went to the town-hall to a dance where I got attracted to a girl and danced, however awkwardly, with her a few times. Dermot Gannon, seeing my interest said, "This is your cousin, Mairead Flynn" —she was a second-cousin on my mother's side—and that was the end of that. Dermot started to go steady with Mairead around that time. I did not cry anymore leaving Ballinamore as it did not have the same effect on me as earlier.

I was going on sixteen then and my hormones were beginning to prosper and I started having wet dreams not knowing what they were, though enjoying them immensely anyway. And it was then that I went to my first dance in Dublin, urged by my mother to go, I think. It was a Sunday and earlier in the day, I went to a Dublin match down the country worrying on the way home, as I was reluctant to go to the dance. It was a hop in Glasnevin Tennis Club—called the Nevin—but I nevertheless plucked up the courage and went. The atmosphere was electric in the thronged hall. There was a four-piece band called the Viscounts and the lead vocalist was Paul Russell with John Curran on the sax. Though I could not put two feet together, I felt there was nothing for it but to have a go. I danced with my sister, Rosemarie a few times to her discomfort and also with Imelda Flanagan. I could not make conversation at all with my dancing partners and after a few pathetic efforts, I would lapse into silence. Still, I enjoyed myself and went every week afterwards, mostly to see the Viscounts, who played every tune to a rock and roll rhythm. We had to go home on the last bus and indeed for as long as I lived in Cabra Road, we would always have to be home by half-eleven.

I did well beyond by own and everybody else's expectations in the Inter in 1960 getting 2157 out of a possible 2400 marks in the five scholarship subjects and getting 97% in Latin. I won a first class Intermediate scholarship achieving twenty-sixth in Ireland thus emulating my brother's success of two years earlier. I got nearly 90% in English and Irish which pleased me very much and 98% in Science, which surprised me. While I did better in Maths, this time it was not as good as my other subjects. Even my father seemed pleased, I am sure, though he was not a proud or vain man.

The decision I took to stay back that year seemed, on the basis of the scholarship success, justified. How was I or anyone else to know that this was the high point of scholastic achievement for me and the road to perdition would start for me in the following summer of 1961.

I did not want to go back to Hugh Jordan's for summer work in 1960 though he came looking for me. Instead, I got a job in a shoddy hotel in Gardiner Street where I worked as a kitchen boy or should I say a slop boy, doing backbreaking work a hundred hours a week for a mere wage of £1. It was then that I learned the value of what my father was trying to do for me in sending me to school. It was here that I came across the coarser things in life for the first time. It was a valuable lesson. I would start at eight in the morning working right through the night. My job was to wash the dishes and scrub the floors and toilets. And sometimes we would have to go upstairs to clean the scum off baths. The used breakfast-trays would come down in a lift and we hungrily eat some of the uneaten food and we would often raid the pantry and gorge ourselves. The owner had married a second time and I overheard him say one night, "I only married her for the ride," talking about his second wife. I got friendly with his children who were as well-mannered as he was crude.

The headwaiter upstairs was Willie and I envied him as he got huge tips at breakfast. He was an orphan and looked like an Italian. I only got a few tips because I was invariably down in the kitchen. Years afterwards, I spent the night in the hotel trying to rekindle the memory of 1960 but it had no affect on me. I wrote a short story about it in 1992 called *Seventeen Revisited* but I did not think it was any good and did not even bother getting it typed. I heard afterwards that the owner who I saw on my revisit had later committed suicide. So money and sex did not make him happy either.

In about May of 1960, I was walking towards the school on a Saturday morning near the bottom of the North Circular Road and I heard a voice bellowing from a house window across the road, "George Rowley, I love you." It was Cora Farrell. This did cartwheels to my ego, and I soon was enthralled with Cora. She was a sister-in-law of Vic Mellowes who was a vocalist in the Charleville Tennis Club where I was to go later.

I used to meet Cora inside the cinema on Saturday or Sunday afternoons but I never actually kissed or even held her hand. I was on the point of phoning her one Saturday night for a date but Donal Galvin persuaded me not to. But deep down, I felt I had not the guts to make the call, fearing rejection. Fear of rejection has been one of my core difficulties all my life and though it is a serious psychological defect, try as I might even with professional help, I have not been able to eliminate it entirely.

On weekdays, myself and Beefy Farrell, renowned as a lady's man and Paddy Murphy would walk up to the North Circular Road and we would meet the girls from Eccles Street Convent. I would chat to Cora and Paddy Murphy was going with Ethel Smith, Cora's pal. Beefy—his Christian name was Dermot—was reputed to be very fast with the women and we looked at him with awe. When he left school, he joined the Gardaí but left the force some years afterwards when he went into the clothing business. He was killed in a car-accident—driving a Merc—before he was thirty. He was literally tall, dark and handsome but overweight, which gave rise to his nickname.

Cora later married Bobby Beckett from Cabra Park and had a few children who must be all grown up by now. But I still remember her holler from the window that Saturday morning which made me feel like a king. Recognition from women still does things to me.

The Olympic Games were held in Rome that year, 1960, and I listened to the races on the radio. Herb Elliot won the 1,500 metres in a canter and Pete Snell from New Zealand won the 800 metres. He was later in 1964 in Tokyo to win the double 800 and 1,500 metres. He was, though lean, built like a tank.

Aunt Nora who was recently widowed, Aunt Mollie and Aunt Kitty, my father's sisters came on a visit in the summer of 1960. A pall of gloom hung over Aunt Nora because of Uncle Jim's death and the visit did not have the same impact on me as the 1958 visit did. I am sure we had parties, but I cannot remember them now.

I do have a photograph of my mother with a cigarette in her mouth with my three aunts. In 1980 when I was on a high because of lack of tablets or too many, I wrote about ten poems, which, in my view, were not great. But the poem, which pleases me most, is called *The Photograph* recalling the photo of my mother in 1960 when she was young, healthy and happy.

> *Time never stands still*
> *But it will in a photograph*
> *The careless laugh of long ago*
> *Not impaired by the ebb and flow*
> *Of time's remorseless ravaging.*

This is a grim piece about my mother's death in sharp contrast to the happiness, however transient, manifest in the actual photograph.

I sent these ten poems to the Irish Times for publication but they were promptly rejected. "Too much jingling to impress," was the cryptic comment.

My Aunt Kitty was married to Tommy Ward, from Galway and loved to talk. He was simple, yet kind. He worked as a bread delivery man in the States but had saved enough to buy a substantial house in Bloomfield, New Jersey near where Auntie Mollie lived. I slept there in Coeyman Avenue when I was in the States in 1982 and I am afraid I got very drunk, something which characterised the whole trip. I have regrets about that to this day which makes me reluctant to go to the States again. Tommy and Aunt Kitty had two children, Marilyn and Irene. I visited Marilyn when I went to the States in 1982.

I went to Ballinamore in August of 1960, and was never again to go there as a teenager. I felt I had outgrown the town by then and had difficulty in passing the time—a feeling of boredom is what I now remember. So I left Dromod Station at the end of August 1960, my future pre-determined in God's creation, as I faced into fifth year. However, as I said earlier I was in fact heading for a dramatic fall from innocence.

In Fifth Year, we had the famous and irrepressible Brother Fitzgerald, "Fitzy", as principal teacher. He taught us Irish and Maths. We had Mr. Carey who was a highly-qualified classical scholar and his books in Latin and English were on the course. He appeared pompous and was always immaculately turned out with his cavalry-twill trousers and high-polished boots. We had Kit Carroll for Applied Maths, who was bald and, though he was a great teacher, he could lose his temper easily but he was not violent. Impatient yes but not violent. It was said of him that the reason he could not get a teaching job at University was that he had a strong Dublin accent. Kit had a great grasp of Maths, Applied Maths and Science, which he brought to other classes. I really enjoyed Applied Maths and, while Maths itself was not my favourite subject, I got an honour in the Leaving in it as well as Applied Maths. Mr. Conlon, a Gaelic speaking native of Rinn, Co. Waterford, taught us Geography. Though he had the subject at his fingertips, he was inclined to be lazy. He would spend the whole class pacing around the room. He broadcast the news in Irish on the radio. He was always referring to my brother Joe's success in getting a university scholarship that year. "Wasn't Geography one of Joe's subjects?" he would get me to confirm to the class. He had a refined and genteel demeanour but we were inclined to make fun of him and mimic his lilting accent. We had Brother Laffan again for Physics and Chemistry, which started to prove more difficult for me after the Inter Cert years.

If Brother Muldowney was an artistic genius, Fitzy in his own way was a genius too. He had an outrageous sense of humour and knew the way of young boys well. He had perfected a system of teaching Irish and Maths and introduced us to French at a later stage, which we all passed in the Leaving. He would block-out the blackboard in vertical columns and select boys to go up and answer questions on their homework. The boys would write vigorously on the board and, when finished, Fitzy would get other boys to read these efforts, as he was half-blind. You would be hoping that a boy of nervous disposition would not be asked to examine your piece. If the boy hesitated at all, you were doomed. Fitzy did not believe in corporal punishment at all but would give penalty exercises for wrongdoing or failure at lessons—"pennos" he would call them. They became often as penal as corporal punishment itself. Fitzy helped Mr. Carey out at Latin and English too and it was not long before we had most of *Macbeth* off by heart. He was hilarious at Latin and could detect when a boy was using a key of slick phrases in doing translations. You would be struggling and would look up at Fitzy to be relieved and he would say "Carry on, I like your style."

One day some boys were up at the board doing their test when Fitzy was called to the phone. Frantic examination of textbooks ensued. When he returned to the room, all he said was "I take it they're correct, gentlemen." What a man. He had not got a mean or capricious bone in his body. He played the violin in the orchestra at the annual opera but was hopeless, much to the frustration of the conductor—Fitzy was so out of tune. Like everything else, he took to the music with great panache. In 1970, he attended my wedding and tried to kiss all the women at the reception. He liked to escape out of the monastery for a drink and when he got old, the brothers had to keep an eye on him. In fact, in later years, he went off to Australia without telling anyone.

When Fitzy died, I went to his funeral. There was a huge attendance, many from St. Vincent's football club, which Fitzy had jointly founded, were there, Kevin Heffernan, Jimmy Keaveney and Tony Hanahoe. But I was there to pay my respects, too. In a moving eulogy, Brother McMahon—"Bottler"—said Fitzy was kissed by more women than anybody and also attended more weddings of old boys and after sixty years in the Christian Brothers, you could pack all his personal belongings into one small suitcase.

Fitzy did not serve his boys for glory or money—most of the Brothers did not—but for service. He was a great man and though he was a Brother, he knew the world well and the wiles of most boys he taught. I also attended Brother Laffan's funeral but there was not the same outpouring of exultation and joy, probably for obvious reasons.

I soon became friends with Arthur McSwiney and Tony Forde and we were friends for years. Arthur lived on the Cabra Road just up from me—his mother had been widowed in 1954 and her husband had had thriving drapery shops in the city but the business went into decline before he died. Mrs. McSwiney was of the old genteel Dublin stock and shared the house with her sister, Mary, who always seemed to need attention, medical or otherwise. There were three boys in Arthur's family and two girls. The mother eked out a living by painting figures on fire-guards or fans, which she sold to Clerys or Arnotts. Dan was the eldest and had to go to work after his father died. Dan worked in the wholesale drapery business and travelled the country. He later serviced the bar trade with cocktail sticks, straws and toilet paper. Dan must have inherited his capacity for hard work from his mother. Our relationship got off to a rocky start but it was still flourishing when my relationship with Arthur began to fade. I admired Mrs. McSwiney immensely and got to feel the same about Dan in later years. Dan had been a promising athlete at school and his daughter Aoife went out with my son Conor in later years. Mark was the youngest brother and became an architect in the Office of Public Works years later where I was working.

Tony Forde and I became best mates too. He was a brilliant student and was raised by his Aunt Nora after his parents went to England. Nora worked as a seamstress in a small shop on North King Street and though they slept in Cooley Road, Drimnagh, they spent most of their time there where Tony did his studying with great effect. These were the days of drainpipe trousers and for a shilling; Nora would take in the bottom of our trousers after our mothers had bought them. I was to learn afterwards that Nora was a highly cultured woman and loved the theatre. We became great friends and she would often visit out home when I got married and my wife was particularly fond of her. Nora and Tony would do their ablutions in the back of the shop where Nora worked. Tony's achievements were great but a lot of it was down to Nora's commitment and her love for him. More of Tony later.

The other boys in the class that I can remember were Jimmy White, very studious, Paddy Devitt was a real genius who was talented at everything and every aspect of athletics and football. Paddy came from a brainy family and his cousins were also famous for their intellectual abilities—one of who got full marks in the Inter in English. Paddy became a priest and still is Professor of Catechetics in Mater Dei Institute. His other cousin John was also in Mater Dei and a teacher of English and a well-known literature and film critic. He is the most well-read man I know but is a bit eccentric and rarely talks, conversation-wise. Billy McPartlin, Joe Murphy and Fergus Cass were all brilliant too but Paddy Devitt, younger than us all, outshone everybody. Though he had great natural intellectual ability, he was very studious. I struggled to hold my own in that class, I can assure you, but in that fifth year at O'Connells, I always got fourth or fifth place. Maybe I make too much of academic achievement but the importance of it was drummed into us from day one and it had huge bearing on my outlook at that point as is evident from what I am recording now. There was no question of cultural worth, for the sole purpose of the system was to get a permanent pensionable job or go to university and pursue an academic career. I think that is what the Brothers felt was their sole mission. I am grateful now that it was the Brothers who taught us the three Rs and introduced us to the wonder of literature, both English and Irish, whatever their motivation. I have to say in their favour, almost without exception, they had the boys' welfare at heart and were very proud of their achievements in Commerce, the Civil Service and University.

To them, yes all of them, I am indeed indebted, despite the methods used by some of the teachers, I can say that sincerely. However as John Devitt said to me a few years ago there were some casualties of the system. I, for one, was one but I had a hand in my own downfall too. For example, my brothers who came through the same system at home and at school came out of it unscathed. Maybe I was over-sensitive but I was somewhat self-indulgent too.

Towards the end of 1960, we were all recruited into the Gilbert and Sullivan light-opera *The Gondoliers* which I enjoyed immensely. This was a fantastic experience though I was only in the chorus. My brother, Gerry, was an understudy for one of the main parts, the Duchess. The boys played the women's parts as well and were completely unabashed doing so. The talent of the leading players was stupendous especially Anthony Glavin who played the comic part of the Duke. He milked it for all it was worth and on the first night and every other night, he brought the house down with his unique and natural talent for comedy. When he left school, he became an established poet and musician. I read recently that he died after a long illness. I loved the rehearsals but getting ready for the first night had a magical feeling—the excitement and the buzz in the dressing rooms, I had never felt before. My parents came one night and were impressed, I think, and at the end of it all we had a celebratory party for all the performers. I performed in the *Pirates* the following year, but *The Gondoliers* was the biggest thrill of all. I was seventeen and as John McGahern said about one of his characters in *Amongst Women*, "I commanded the world." We did not have to study hard in fifth year and it was a bazz. In January 1961, Mr. Conlon announced, *as Gaeilge*, "There is a Kennedy now in the White House and another Kennedy, Ambassador to Nigeria who had been a pupil in O'Connells". Up to then, we had not taken much interest in world or political affairs. I, for one, confined myself to sports events, athletics, boxing and Gaelic football, but JFK becoming president of the USA fired all our imaginations that morning in January 1961 as Spike paced around the room. Within three years, Kennedy was assassinated by a sniper in Dallas, Texas.

PART THREE
1961–1970

I N JANUARY 1961, ARTHUR AND I DECIDED that we would go
to England to work during the summer, just out of the blue.
Nothing would shake us from this resolve and so we wrote
to Bird's Eye Foods, Smedley's and to Westwick Frosted Foods
in Norfolk, where we eventually got a job in the pea-factory.
We looked forward to it with great expectation though it was
unheard of at that time that boys who were not at University
would to go to work in the pea-factories. My brother, Joe, was
also to get a job that summer in another part of Norfolk.

I sailed through the rest of the school year, nearly eighteen,
and my whole life ahead of me and I had no inhibitions about
the future. Just before we broke up for the holidays, Fitzy offered
me a job helping the Supervisor at the exams but I refused, as I
was hell-bent and unwavering in my desire to go to England.
My father, a wise man, knew I was at a tender and vulnerable
age but I was insistent, and he eventually agreed to let me go.
We had been accepted for work at Westwick Frosted Foods near
North Walsham in Norfolk. Nothing could go wrong.

We left on the mail-boat on Friday, June 10, 1961 and my

father, still objecting, gave me the fare and a fiver pocket money. "Make sure to write," my mother said, "and say your prayers." She was weeping but I was elated as I got on the mailboat at Dun Laoghaire, which was thronged with emigrants, most of them permanently leaving for England for work. The savage emigration of the fifties had not yet started to abate. Many on board were drunk and were still singing sad ballads as we arrived at Holyhead at one in the morning to immediately board the train for London. So keyed up as I was, I could only fitfully sleep and I would peer out the window marvelling at the red postboxes and thinking—this is the life at last. I must have had an inferiority complex about Ireland and all things Irish; I was so overwhelmed by my first experience of the exotic. The Brothers had instilled in us the love of family and the hatred of everything English, the true definition of patriotism. The real heroes were those who died for Irish freedom or so the Brothers said.

We arrived in London at about 7:00 AM and at the station, I was greeted by a cockney porter, "Cheer up, Mate," recognition at last. Arthur and I got a train to Norwich, where we had lunch and got a bus to the factory, which was in what seemed a wilderness. It was all new to me and I felt a huge sense of anticipation as we had our dinner—a big fry in the factory canteen, trying to avoid paying.

We went to our sleeping quarters, which were a long workers' billet with beds lined on either side with nothing but rough blankets for covering and a pillow. On the Saturday evening after we had our dinner, the factory manager came to us in the billet and said, "Make sure to pay the girl." Most of my co-workers were university students and we tried to bluff it that we were at university too but not succeeding. I was fearful that we might not be taken on the Monday on that account—fear racked my soul.

We awoke refreshed on Sunday and I said to Arthur, "We'll have to go to Mass." I was still a very devout Catholic and regarded missing Mass as a mortal sin. We walked the five miles to

North Walsham and back, the spacious Norfolk Broads alongside the road, with pleasure-boats in abundance.

On Monday morning when we reported to the Office for
work we were questioned about our age and we lied, for Arthur
was a year younger than me but we got a job on the day-shift
which did not pay as well as I was hoping. But we soon got a
better job where the rates were higher on the nightshift at five
shillings an hour working from eight until eight. Our job was
to take the peas from the freezer, and having graded them, to
put them in boxes. Even in the first week, I was struck by a most
powerful feeling of homesickness, and I cried in bed much to the
amusement of my co-workers. The homesickness was as palpable
as it was profound and was to last for the whole of my stay at
Westwick. The foremen wore pink hats and were fair as long as
we did our work. I would go down to the canteen to see if there
was a letter from home. My mother was to write regularly as I
did. "Make sure you say your prayers," she would write, "and
don't work too hard. And go to Mass, don't forget – Daddy sends
his love. Xxx Mam."

My first week's wages—£25— seemed to make it all worthwhile. I promptly went up to North Walsham to send £20 home
to my mother by registered post. My father would still have been
giving her £10 a week so this would have been a fortune to her
and it was. It is not for the purposes of this memoir to analyse
why I would want to work my summer holidays and give most
of my wages to my mother but most boys did at that time. Maybe I felt it a duty. We were enjoined at school to love our parents
and we would be as dutiful as Christ was to Mary and Joseph.
It should be said that £5 per week, which I kept for myself, was
ample for my needs. I immediately saw the uselessness of money
beyond one's needs. So I got by fine on £5 per week.

For the first week, before we got paid, we would survive on
strawberries from the fields and dry bread—though some of the
lads looked for a sub and got it. The freezer was as cold as the
Arctic and I did not relish going in there with my light clothes.

Like I said, most of the lads were university students from Kerry and Mayo, and during breaks we would talk about football and religion. They soon got to know that I was very religious and they would rib me a lot about it. In fact, one night, I went into the freezer and found a page three pin-up of a nude woman stuck on the pea trolley. It was good-hearted fun, though and I enjoyed, otherwise, the banter. We would put the frozen peas on a conveyor belt until they dropped into cardboard boxes for dispatch. One of the foremen was George with his pink cap and he would come around from time to time to check-up on us but otherwise the supervision was minimal. At 8:00 AM we would clock-out and after breakfast, a huge fry, we would head for bed to sleep the sleep of the just.

But then came the dramatic change in my life, which was to affect me adversely for many years. Adversely is an understatement in the light of what was to soon happen in Westwick—catastrophically would be closer to the mark.

In the second week, a terrible reality was born, or should I say emerged, in my psyche.

We finished the shift, as usual, and went to breakfast exhausted from the night's work. I went to bed under the coarse blanket and promptly fell asleep. I never had trouble sleeping even when I was an altar boy; I would just conk out and sleep through the night. About twelve noon on that day, I was woken by some of the lads playing cards and laughing at the end of the billet. For the life of me, I could not get back to sleep. Even though forty-five years have passed since then, I still remember the exact moment when the obsession that I could not get back to sleep, began. I recognised it instantly that it was an obsession, which was to keep me awake then and for many years to come. Like all obsessions, it became a vicious circle—the more I tried to get to sleep by concentrating on more benign thoughts the more the obsession asserted itself. The obsession kept me awake all that day and when I got out of bed about five o'clock, I was in turmoil. All through the night-shift, I was afraid that I would not get to sleep the next day, which tortured me. I started speaking to the lads about it and some of them said a few pints would make you sleep. I went to bed as usual that week and slept only for an hour or two, the troubled sleep of the insomniac. As I lay in bed awake, my head in chaos, I started to think what if I never slept with the Leaving Cert year ahead of me in September. I became rooted with fear. I decided that if I went on to the day-shift, this would restore my sleeping pattern. A night-shift of twelve hours could be too much for a boy of seventeen. I went on to day-shift though the wages were not as good but I would have done anything to get back to normal. But this strategy did not work at all and the obsession continued unabated and my distress became more acute. One evening in early July, I had finished my work, had my dinner, and was sitting on my bed when some of the lads said they were going down to Worsted village for a drink and invited me along. "Maybe it will help you sleep," one of them said, "if you had a few pints." I agreed to go with them, though I had never tasted alcohol before. There was no drinking culture in our home when I was growing up except at parties and, as I told you, my father never went to the pub for which I am still grateful.

Worsted is a small village about a mile from the factory and has given its name to the tweed. We arrived at the pub—a few Trinity students and me and when I was asked what I was having, I did not know what to order. I was about to break my confirmation pledge and this was a big occasion for me. One of the lads said, "Try a pint of Carlsberg that's what I'm having." So I had had a pint of Carlsberg and the duck took to the water at seventeen until the duck could no longer quack at forty-one. I did not feel it a momentous occasion or of any great significance but the ice was broken as regards alcohol. I had two more pints of Carlsberg that night and felt so giddy, I attempted to kick a cat with glee on the way back to our base. I slept a little better, though fitfully, but the dominant thought about not being able to get sufficient sleep persisted. I felt so bad one evening, I went to see a doctor who gave me some tablets but they did not work either and I began to panic. I was still doing twelve-hour shifts by day and sending money home—writing to my mother saying I was fine. Round about that time, we moved to a country-house beside the seaside town of Cromer, with comfortable beds and proper linen. But even these improved surroundings did not abate the insomnia. I did not know what way to turn; I decided that the only thing to do was to go home, though I knew this would disappoint my parents especially my mother. But I felt it was a crisis and was convinced that if I got home to familiar terrain, my sleeping pattern would return to normal and I would be able to rest up for the Leaving Cert year. I did not know it then but I knew it later and am more convinced about it now, no matter where you go you bring your troubles with you. You could not run, you have to stand your ground. But I was convinced that leaving Westwick was the solution to my problems. So I went to the Office to get the balance of my pay and a refund of my travelling expenses. I got about fifty pounds I think. In all, I had lasted a month in Westwick Frosted Foods and said goodbye to Arthur who remained for the rest of the summer. I boarded the train for London at Norfolk and, if not broken, I was shattered in sharp contrast to my happy demeanour when I arrived. When I got to London, I sent a telegram to my parents to say I was on my way home not elaborating but telling them not to worry. I passed the Tower of London, Big Ben, and the Houses of Parliament and though my mind was in disarray, I marvelled at them knowing them only previously from news-reels. As I walked around, a motor cavalcade with Yuri Gagarin passed by waving triumphantly to the crowd. I spent the whole day wandering around the West End and Piccadilly and marvelled at the advertising hoardings for the various strip-shows where, outside, the bouncers would try to entice the punters in. But I decided not to venture in as I thought it would be a mortal sin to deliberately go to a strip show. So I killed time until I boarded the train from Euston to Holyhead chastened but hopeful that the end of my troubles was in sight but they were only just beginning, a series of events that was to culminate in total disintegration in eight years time. It was a slow painful process up to then and a gradual process too but the train was heading for the precipice and I did not have the resources within me or the professional help to get off.

As the boat was reaching Dublin Bay, I saw the Dublin Brendan Behan immortalised in *The Borstal Boy* on his return from jail in England. I boarded the train for Westland Row, wondering what kind of a reception my parents would give me —if not quite frosty, it would not be a *Cead Mile Failte* either. On my way up to O'Connell Street, I met my brother, Gerry, who was cycling to his work in Hugh Jordan's and Gerry was all agog as to why I had left England. I tried to explain but realised it was useless. When I arrived home after a perfunctory welcome, I tried to tell my mother what had happened but she threw her eyes up to heaven not wanting to know, not to mention understand. There was no word of sympathy, no talk of doctors, just a blanket refusal to accept that I was in turmoil. I gave her £20 of my £50 more to clear my conscience. I am not saying my father was furious when he came home but he was definitely confused. How could I possibly have given up such a good job—it was beyond his comprehension. No word of sympathy or understanding of my plight. No word of concern about my insomnia and the reasons for it. I felt it futile to explain.

But I was optimistic that I could now sleep but this proved groundless. Though I could sleep a bit more than in Norfolk, the most I could manage was a fitful tossing and turning and this continued for the rest of the summer. Meanwhile, I got a job in Hugh Jordan's for a pittance compared to Westwick, working alongside Gerry—always cheerful, always optimistic. I wrote to Arthur with an apology for leaving when I did and he wrote back a long Joycean type of reply, which seemed to me to be very clever.

The £30 I had left burned a hole in my pocket and one or

two nights I would go the Brian Boru pub at Cross Guns Bridge and have a few pints of Guinness for the first time ever. I was immediately smitten by the bitter taste but three was my limit and I would eat a bag of crisps as well. The Guinness set my head reeling in bed at night and the obsession abated as I dozed off, only to awaken hours later with my mind going like a furnace. Basically, the geographical return to Ireland, while it helped a little, as well as the Guinness, did not deal with the basic problem. This pattern continued for the rest of the summer. I would go, though not all evenings, to the Brian Boru, followed by a very disturbed sleeping pattern. By day, the obsession, which had driven me out of England, was getting worse and worse. Surely, I should have sought medical advice or counselling or even psychiatric help—which was taboo then. My parents did not want to know anything that would trouble them. After all, they had six others to look after and their hands were full. However, if I had sought help, as a last resort, and if that failed what then would I do. So I decided to endure the pain and faced into my Leaving Cert year in that frame of mind—completely unprepared psychologically for the hard grind that would be. It seemed that I was defeated, for how could I continue to study with my mind in such turmoil—and no balm to hand. But that year I proved to be more durable than I thought I could be.

There was great excitement in the schoolyard before going into class for our last year in O'Connells—such enthusiasm—but try as I might, I could not share in it. We had the same teachers as for fifth year. The pattern of the past few weeks continued and my studying suffered which the teachers began to notice from the tests they were giving us. Towards the end of December, we went on a retreat and literally disgraced ourselves drinking in Campion's Pub and putting puerile questions in the question box. So annoyed was the priest in charge that he summoned Brother O'Connell to the retreat house, who warned us that if this behaviour continued we would be expelled. One thing the school authorities did when organising the retreats was to separate the boys who were pals. So some of the boys went to Rathfarnham Castle. Our retreat ended on the Friday but a few of us, Arthur, Tony and others, decided to cross the city and go to Rathfarnham and stay the night and join the other boys for breakfast. Bets were laid that we would not have the nerve to do this daring thing. So we headed for Rathfarnham but in town we stopped for a few pints and were a little merry when we arrived at the Castle. It was too early to go in so we went for a few more pints in Rathfarnham village intending to return to the castle later. We were a little tipsy by then and we started to place roadblocks in the middle of the road and were about to walk away when a Garda came up beside us on a motorbike and wrote down our names and addresses. Arthur and Tony were still with me at that stage. Thinking fast, I gave my address as 75 Phibsboro Road, Cabra. Some weeks later Arthur and Tony got summonses but I got none. One evening, I was doing my homework in the dining room when a knock came to the door and I went to answer it. It was a plainclothes detective and he asked to see George Rowley. "Senior or Junior?" I asked. He asked me how old I was and I said eighteen. The detective said he had come to warn me if there were a repeat of the incident in Rathfarnham, we would not get off so lightly. Apparently, Arthur's sister worked in Charlie Haughey's company who was the Minister of Justice and Charlie arranged for the charges to be dropped. Then the detective asked to see my father to give me the warning in his presence. I appealed to his sympathies. I said my father had just come out of hospital after a hernia operation and the news that I had been in trouble would affect his recovery. So the detective let the matter stand as it was and I escaped with a caution. What relief; you can only imagine what my father's reaction would have been especially with the question of drink being involved. My father did not know I drank until a few years later—it was definitely taboo in 1961.

At school, my performance continued to decline and even involvement in the opera, *The Pirates of Penzance,* did little to lift my gloom. But I went into it anyway and was notable by the fact that Fitzy persuaded me to dress up as a Bean Garda for the policeman's chorus, which I did completely, upstaging the Sergeant's *A Policeman's Lot is not a Happy One*. He was not pleased.

At the Christmas exam, I had slipped to near the bottom of the class and Fitzy raised the matter of withholding the balance of the money from the Intermediate scholarship on this account. But I appealed to him and my mother got the money. In fifth year, I had always got in the first five and to slip down to the bottom was remarkable and let me say with all the objectivity I can muster, it was not the drink, and it was definitely the insomnia caused by the obsession I had since the summer. Surely, the alarm bells should have been ringing loud and clear but nobody did anything to establish what the root of the problem was. So I faced into 1962, the Leaving Cert exam year and I decided that I was going to fail the exam so there was no point in doing it anyway. So I determined to sneak off to England at Easter and get a job there, a bleak future for an erstwhile studious boy.

But fate again took a hand. Just before Easter, Tony Forde said to me in the corridor, "Carey is going to die," which left me nonplussed. He explained to me that he and Michael Ryan, a classmate, were going to put Mr. Carey's death notice in the papers as a prank and would I like to be involved. I needed no persuasion. We discussed it further and it was arranged that Tony's girlfriend would be the one to make the calls to the newspapers pretending that she was ringing from an undertaker. Well, it worked and the "death notice" appeared in all three dailies on Friday, 13 April 1962. I recall Mr. Carey being called to the phone when the news broke and the consternation, which followed. Though most of the boys were not privy to our involvement, Billy McPartland guessed as we had asked him for Carey's address—both of them lived in Rathfarnham. The matter was made worse by the fact that Carey was not living with his wife at the time so imagine her shock when she saw the papers. The Principal teacher Brother O'Connell responded quickly, summoning all the boys from Carey's classes for interview in the monastery. I was cool as the proverbial cucumber and did not blink an eye, nor did Tony nor Michael Ryan. But unknown to us Billy unwittingly spilled the beans on us and after Easter I was playing football up the lane—the school had been agog about the incident and the Brothers were keeping sharp eye on everybody—when two policemen called to the house looking for me and I was called frantically by Gerry. I first denied involvement, my father defending me when I faltered, when questioned. But I eventually confessed to the anguish of my parents. My father in particular was aghast, went straight to bed, and lapsed into total silence. You see up to then, I had been a paragon of good and studious behaviour and it was certainly a tremendous shock to all my family. The Brothers had no choice but to expel us as the teachers' union was putting on pressure. So, towards the end of April 1962, I left O'Connells in disgrace. One of the policemen who arrested us was Mr. Devitt, a Garda Inspector who was John Devitt's father. John and I often laugh about it now. We had to go to Fitzgibbon Street Garda Station to make a statement and the Guards asked us about a similar prank, which happened in relation to Brother Laffan the previous year. Though all three of us had been involved the notice was not in fact published. We all denied any involvement and got away with it. We walked out of the Garda Station and went our separate ways—my relationship with Michael Ryan was never to recover.

The gloom over Cabra Road can be easily understood—my father especially transfixed in silence—the idea that his son could be charged with something like this appalled him as the good name of the family which he had cultivated all these years lay in ruins. A pall of despair descended on the house. After about a week, my father asked, "What are you going to do now?" "Well," I blurted out, "I am not going to do the Leaving." I was determined about that.

My father went down to the school to appeal my expulsion and was met by Brother O'Connell, the Principal, who stood firm. "But what about the boys' welfare?" my father said. "I don't care about the boys' welfare, spiritual or temporal," he replied. My father was so annoyed he was going to return the money, which Joe got, when he received the award for best boy in 1960 but eventually he decided to keep it. For some reason, I changed my mind and decided to do the Leaving Certificate after all. The Brothers would not let me sit the exam in the school so I had to arrange with the Department of Education to do it at another venue—the O'Lehane Hall in Parnell Square, the offices of the Union of Distributive Workers and Clerks, now Mandate. So I decided to study and make up for lost time. I could relax a bit more now, as I did not have the pressure of getting up in the morning to go to school. This eased the obsession somewhat, though it still persisted. The enormity of what had happened at Easter did not mitigate the insomnia completely. I still could only manage a few hours sleep with the aid of a few pints of Guinness once or twice a week. So that early summer, I studied in the back garden like a demon—I had all the notes and the class would only be doing revision now so I felt that I was not at too great a disadvantage. My mother used to peer out of her bedroom window at me and she was delighted. I loved poetry and my favourite poems were Shelley's *Stanzas Written in Dejection near Naples* and *Ode to the West Wind*. "I fall upon the thorns of life I bleed"—how I identified with that. I loved Keats as well and still could master Latin and Applied Maths. Thanks be to God for the teachers' notes which I had assiduously taken down verbatim—despite the continual drama being played out in my head, I could still memorise! I did eight subjects in the Leaving Cert and went dutifully to the O'Lehane Hall where invariably, I was the only one doing Honours—the pink paper. I made a mess of the English paper from the very start and knew I would not get an honour in it. As the day went on, my performance on the paper got worse and worse because the bad start had unnerved me. The insomnia got quite brutal during the three weeks of the Leaving Cert and most nights I did not sleep at all, not even fitfully. But somehow, I kept going and the last day was Applied Maths and I was the only one doing it—I half-apologised to the supervisor for this.

Arthur had left school in January for some reason unknown to me, which was regarded as a mystery. I met him and Tony in the Brian Boru on the last day for a few pints of Guinness, having the wherewithal by selling our schoolbooks in Fred Hanna's. I came home a bit light in the head and if my parents noticed anything, they said nothing. They were pleased that I had done the exam, all eight subjects.

Early in 1962, I had started going with Doreen Oman, a voluptuous well-endowed girl from Stanhope Street Convent where my sisters Anne and Mollie were attending. Indeed, it was Anne who brought the note to Doreen from me saying that I would like a date. We would go to the pictures on Sunday afternoon and sit in the back-row courting passionately, though just kissing. Doreen did not like petting though she seemed very experienced at kissing which aroused me greatly. When news got out that we had been expelled from school, it became a *cause célèbre* amongst our school-going peers. Doreen was impressed but she said, "What did your parents say?" I have always regarded, even then, getting expelled from school as a blessing in disguise because I now could study without external pressure. Otherwise, I would have gone to England defeated in despair.

I went with Doreen until June but then I met the first real love of my life, Orla Donoghue. She was Brendan Donoghue's sister who had been in my class in fifth and sixth year. He was a gifted footballer and hurler, later playing for Dublin and was an accomplished athlete. I liked him a lot but I was not at that point as close to him as I was with Tony and Arthur. His father was a hard-working postman and also a strong Union man and he his wife and four daughters and Brendan lived in Charleville Avenue near O'Connells. I met Orla almost by accident on a double-date with her sister Noeleen who was going with Tony Forde. Orla and I were really only making up a foursome, but I fell for her at once. We went to Charleville Tennis Club that first night and I really got aroused when she got close. Vic Mellowes was lead vocalist and Brian Dooley who later became an architect in the OPW was the jazz pianist, with a cigarette almost dropping from his lips as he belted out *Kiddio*, singing it in a gravelly voice.

I walked Orla home as she wheeled her bike and we arranged to meet the following Saturday. Tony had long since disappeared with Noeleen, going down to her house for a "curte". I was too shy to kiss Orla the first night, though she asked me in. I met her the next Saturday on her own this time, but first we went to the Brian Boru—Orla was only sixteen and did not drink but I had a few pints of Guinness. When Brendan heard this afterwards he was furious but I held my ground. I then started to see Orla regularly and we would go to the pictures and for walks holding hands and kissing innocently. Orla was beautiful in appearance and manner and I was happy. Needless to say Doreen found out about my two-timing and said she did not want to see me again and that was that. I did not give a damn about Doreen now, I was so besotted with Orla. But joy is a transient thing and one night after the pictures, she broke it off without explanation though I thought we were doing well together. I was heart-broken and when I asked Brendan why she had ended the relationship, he said she felt I was too intense and serious which she could not hack, with all my talk about religion, he said. I was taken completely by surprise as I always thought I had a great sense of humour. I was flattened by this rejection and would identify with sad songs about unrequited love for weeks afterwards.

I was scheduled to sit the Junior Executive Officer exam in July and the exam was based on the courses I had done for the Leaving Cert Honours, but the standard was much higher. I did not hold out much hope but I studied all the same from my notebooks. The Custom and Excise Officers examination was also incorporated in this exam—it was for students in their nineteenth year, which I was. The Exam was much more difficult than the Leaving and I felt I had not a chance but it was in my nature to have a go and I did. One night as I was studying, I listened to the World Cup Final between Brazil and Czechoslovakia, which Brazil won with Pele being a leading light. I was thrilled.

After the exam I got a job in a Parkgate Street Photographers for £5 a week; the proprietor was a Mr. Hodges whose daughter Emer, I knew. There were five boys, my own age, developing and printing photographs—it was the busy season. I enjoyed the work and was put in charge of the accounts. Most of the lads were working-class and had left school at fourteen. They were rough and gentle at the same time. I used to have to deliver messages to various shops and enjoyed getting out and about. Though I did not smoke, you could only have a smoke in the dark room. There was an older guy there, Dessie, and we would often go to the a local pub after work for a few pints and it would be only a few and I became convinced that they would help me to sleep better. I had by then adopted the tactic of going to bed early but that did not work either—I would be wide-awake at two in the morning but I would still get up for work the following day.

I knew the Leaving Results would come out in August and I became fretful about this. I went down to the school on the due date, and met Paddy Devitt who kindly helped in looking for my results. I asked a Brother for my results in writing but he only typed them on a blank sheet of paper. Both my father and I were furious about this—it still rankles with me today. I had mixed feelings about my results, though I got five honours. I was disappointed in particular about my English result in which I only got 214 of a possible 400. But I knew that I had done badly anyway. My father, however, was convinced that Mr. Carey had influenced the examiners—what a simple man! Though my parents were pleased, I cried bitter tears because, based on my Inter

Cert results and given normal progression, I should have got a University scholarship. But I acknowledged then and now that it was a great achievement given the chaos in my head. I feel that more strongly today and better was to come. The results of the Junior Executive Officer exam for entry into the Civil Service came out in September 1962 as well as the Customs and Excise outcome. I did relatively well by my exacting standards. I got 72nd in Ireland in the Junior Executive Officer exam and 26th place in the Customs and Excise exam and I had a decent chance of being called to either. I first got called to the Customs and Excise and I did all the preliminaries—Irish and Medical exams and was on the point of being offered a position but my mother did not like this option as she did not want me to be assigned to the country where she feared I would get too fond of drink for want of something better to do in my spare time in a remote part of the country. However, my luck turned again and I got a letter from the Civil Service Commission in O'Connell Street asking me to call to see them. I went with trepidation, fearing I was not getting appointed to the Custom's job, which I was hellbent on taking. The official I met had great and unexpected news for me—would I like a position of Junior Executive Officer? I was overwhelmed but not enough to say yes immediately. "I would have to speak with my mother," I told the perplexed official. I ran the whole way home and blurted out my news to my mother. She was as excited as I was. "I knew my prayers would be answered," she said.

About mid-November, I got official word that I was being assigned to the Office of Public Works starting 24 January 1963. Despite all my tribulations in 1961 and 1962, I was now headed for the future, my star in the ascendancy. I thanked God I had not gone to England to take a dead-end job—no future, no outlet. I had fulfilled my parents' dream; it seemed my luck had turned.

The job at Hodges had finished in October. He was very reluctant to let me go but there was no more work. I soon got a sales job in the Jordan Dexter agency selling venetian blinds. And boy, was I a good salesman with verbal agility and a well-honed sales pitch. We would be dropped off in a Dublin housing estate and I would soon get into the charm offensive with un-suspecting housewives and I did very well at it. The managers of the agency, two brothers would measure the windows and later install the blinds. I opted for a basic wage and 5% commission as I felt I would do well selling and I did. On a good week I would earn about £10 and give my mother £5. The job was to last up to Christmas, which suited me as I was entering the Civil Serv-ice in January 1963. Towards the end of my term in the job, I got very drunk with my colleagues having bet them that I could drink eight pints and, after I did, a row started between us. Also, I was assaulted on the way home, an assault which I did not pro-voke. I slipped into the house quietly, my parents being in bed.

The 24th January 1963 arrived and an all-embracing hope took me to its bosom. I had no inhibitions or fears about my ability. The previous week my parents had visited Syl Fitzsimons in St. Vincent's Hospital which was then located on the east side of St. Stephen's Green beside the opw. After their visit, they went down to the Office and, as God is my judge, they said a prayer of thanks for my success. Though a lot of my generation, coming from humble backgrounds went into the Civil Service, my father regarded it as a first for the family to get a permanent and pensionable job working for the Irish Government in a free Ireland. His brothers had fought in the War of Independence and he had been raised on an eight-acre farm in Leitrim from where most of the family had to emigrate. So it was a proud day for both my parents and hard work and ambition would surely propel their son to the top. My father was grateful too that there was no need for "pull", the scourge of the working classes that had no influence in commerce or insurance. Indeed Gerry, my brother and my sisters, Anne and Mollie later joined the Civil Service, Rosemarie went into the Agricultural Institute, a semi-state body and Noreen, the youngest, became a teacher. Of the family, Joe was the only who went into business, setting up his own chemical company and became very successful.

There was ice on the steps as I went into the OPW the first morning and I was brought to see Paddy Kearney, the Personnel Officer, who after a brief chat said they would keep me in Personnel on the industrial side. I was introduced to my first boss, a Higher Executive Officer, Mita Hastings and kind and hardworking she was too. I was put sitting opposite Hugh Malone, a fat moon-faced fellow in his thirties, which seemed ancient to me. A huge pile of files on my table nearly blocked Hugh from view. We talked for a while and then he shocked me by saying, "Get out of this dump as soon as you can." Kitty Murphy, a matronly Clerical Officer in her fifties sat behind me and became very helpful. Bridie Reilly was a Clerical Assistant and I can remember well her outrageous mini-skirt and high heels. I was in no way intimidated by the huge pile of files and was full of confidence. After I was just a fortnight in Personnel, I was assigned to another section across the room—Controller, Districts Maintenance Division. It had nothing to do with my performance but a personality clash in the other division. I did not mind the transfer one bit and I soon settled in. Michael Corcoran was my boss, a strict Higher Executive Officer who would always come in with a rolled umbrella and the Irish Independent. He was a precise, highly regarded Official but was fair and a stickler for accuracy. But he put me through my paces with kindness and great deliberation. In short, he was the perfect boss for a newcomer with his efficiency and capacity for hard work.

Pauline Gilmartin, from Mayo, who sat behind Michael, was the typist. She was then in her thirties and was devoted to her mother who was ill which necessitated Pauline going home at weekends. I was assistant to the Controller and the work did not stretch me, as it was merely the recording of payments on a blue card for school building projects. I had no doubt but that I would master it and I did.

We got paid on the sixteenth and the last day of the month,

and got the cheque the day before. I gave my mother half my wages, £16 for the half month and was to continue to look after her financially until I got married in 1970 but the proportion of my salary got less when I started to save for marriage. There was a banking facility in nearby Ely Place where I cashed my first cheque though most of the staff went to O'Dwyers of Leeson Street at the junction with St. Stephen's Green where you could cash the cheque the day before the actual payday. But I was not to start doing this until Easter.

When I told my father, what Hugh Malone had said about poor promotion prospects in the Office my father dismissed this as bitterness on his part.

Further up the room was Paddy McMahon, a tall handsome man in his thirties from Clare and Sean Barrett his boss, and further up was Paddy Condon who was to become a big influence on me later particularly from the point of view of union activities. Paddy was in his forties then and was in the army during the war. He indeed had a military bearing walking like a sergeant-major. I remember one Saturday morning his walking briskly down the room to me, his arms going like pistons, and he said "You'll join the union, will you?" in his no-nonsense way that I was soon to get used to. Knowing that there was no point in demurring I said yes immediately. Later that year, I was co-opted on to the Branch Committee and this began a service-long involvement with union matters. I was completely idealistic which I am sure was typical of young people at the time. I later got disillusioned and bitter because of what I thought was lack of principle and honour amongst union ranks. I learned that promotion prospects were poor—there were about forty-five eligible executive officers with very little prospect of promotion and there was a very active campaign for Equalisation of Promotional Opportunities service-wide which lead to bitter conflict with Departments who had good prospects. In some pay periods, you had to suffer three weekends without pay but at the end of the quarter there was a bonanza after tax.

It was Easter Saturday and we got our pay-cheques, cashable the Tuesday after the bank holiday, but I could not afford to wait that long. I went up to O'Dwyers with Paddy Condon who introduced me to Joe, the proprietor—a gruff man from Co. Tipperary, whose family owned a number of pubs in Dublin, having started from scratch. After a little grumbling, Joe was persuaded by Paddy to cash my cheque and I proceeded to get drunk on Guinness and vodka, drinking quickly in an effort to impress Paddy and the rest of the lads who had also cashed their cheques. For years afterwards I cashed my cheque in O'Dwyers and it was like a Las Vegas casino on payday, with Billy Twyford the manager in charge. Billy was kind but his no-nonsense approach kept order. I soon got to know Colm Jackson, a great raconteur from Belfast, Sean Barrett, a principled union man, Brendan O'Hehir, Johnny Doyle etc. etc. Colm was master of ceremonies and ensured everybody got a hearing but he could not tolerate shoptalk. I was enthralled by the witty banter and jokes, mainly clean, and references to literature. O'Dwyers was to become a regular haunt of mine and I held my own in conversation and wit. If you did not like what I said, I would quickly let you know it and I soon had the reputation for quick-fire repartee. Just short of being a nuisance. But I think I became a bit of a nuisance in later years and some people started to avoid me if I had been drinking a lot. I elevated the drinkers of O'Dwyers to iconic status because of their legendary drinking capacity and I longed to become one of them. Though we went to the best school in Ireland where true values were instilled in us, we came out of it with no value system at all. Our revolution was to stop going to Mass (which I had), question everything and become left-wing, which I tried hard to be. And of course becoming seasoned drinkers but being able to carry it.

I soon was spending all my money on drink and would be broke before payday, then resorting to borrowing. First ten shillings and then a pound. It was to become a habit and an obvious danger sign that drink was becoming my master. However my parents did not seem to notice as I always gave my mother her money and would never in any circumstance borrow from her. But it seemed that borrowing was habitual for a lot of people in the OPW in these early years especially amongst the porters. One of them, a precise, bespeckled dainty man—I cannot recall his name, would borrow a half-a-crown from me regularly. You could get a pint for one shilling and ten pence then. Most of the porters were old IRA men, politically appointed. Big Paddy Devitt, a giant of a man but who was childlike and Bob Doyle who was inarticulate, drunk or sober, and shuffled along, appearing ready to fall at any moment. But they were all great characters and would join us in O'Dwyers after work. There was never an element of social snobbery in the job and we all mixed well.

Though I was now drinking more heavily, I was still going to the pictures and had started going to plays with the encouragement of Paddy McMahon. One evening, when I was not long in the job, I went to a film in the Carlton opposite the Savoy and saw a film *The Premature Burial* by Edgar Allan Poe with Ray Milland in the lead role. He became obsessed with the idea that he would be buried alive, triggered off by the air of the song *Molly Malone*. He thought he had developed the disease of catilepsy, a condition that you are in such a state of unconsciousness that you have all the appearances of being dead. He was convinced that he had been inflicted with this disease though he had not it at first. But he was to develop it later such was the intensity of his obsession. He is in fact to be buried alive but he climbs out of his grave from a purpose-made coffin and runs, terrified, from the cemetery. This film so affected me that my head was in turmoil and I began to obsess that I too had catilepsy. The obsession lasted for weeks keeping me awake at night and I soon became convinced that I too had developed the condition solely by virtue of thinking that I had it, just like Milland. Now I had something tangible to worry about and I became distraught with fear. As a last resort, I turned to prayer and went to a retreat in Rathfarnham Castle for peace and quiet.

In confession, I told the priest everything and he did his best to comfort me but to no avail.

I was wrecked going into work after the weekend retreat, which did no good at all, only to be greeted by Michael Corcoran: "Did we have a good weekend?" Michael was always on time but had no style. The obsession continued for weeks with its attendant insomnia so I drank more and more to numb the pain, setting in place a classical vicious circle, which I could not break. I began to get lines under my eyes and to feel continually tired which worried me as I gazed into the mirror.

One man who became my friend and mentor that year was Fergus Gilmore. He was a colossus and intellectual genius but also became a great friend. He had gone to O'Connells where he excelled and was set for a career in engineering but his father had died young and Fergus joined the Civil Service in 1952. I first met him in the corridor of the Office and we got talking, and I told him I went to O'Connells and he replied, "Why aren't you wearing the school tie?" "Oh, I wouldn't do that," I replied to which he retorted, "So you have become cynical." Fergus was a man apart and did not drink like the regulars in O'Dwyers but became an icon for me and I revered him, which was warranted. He was an accomplished cricket player—he played for the Leinster Cricket Club in Rathmines and was capped for Leinster in tennis. I began to worship him and he was to have a huge influence on me. He came from a completely different background from me. Some would call him West Brit. He hated the IRA with a passion and often teased me for my leanings towards that organisation. He was blessed with a caustic and ironic wit and was exceedingly well read, his passion being the Second World War. He started to give me lifts home at lunch-hour on his way to Glasnevin where he lived—though in his thirties he was still a bachelor and a lively one at that. He had plenty of lady admirers though at heart he was a man's man. He loved the company of his fellow cricketers. He was to become my boss in 1968/69 and was inspirational. I craved his company but though he liked a pint and could handle it, he did not make a habit of it, which I respected and never once did he tell me that I was drinking too much. We were to become great friends but I never felt equal to him, being in awe to his laconic wit and turn of phrase. He could cut you down in a flash with a caustic comment though he was very kind to me. We would meet in Madigans of Earl Street, a great Guinness house and I would be flattered by his attention, feeling despair if somehow he could not make it. We would go to the Metropole or Clerys Ballroom, after the pub and he could turn on a sixpence. He was to witness the horror of my mental collapse in 1969 first-hand and made vain efforts to get me to go to hospital, something I would not do because I was so completely adrift from reality, wired to the moon with no prospect of getting back to "terra firma". But I will deal with this later. The chronology with which I am writing this memoir helps my memory.

At Easter 1963, I first met Connie Langan, a robust country-girl from North County Dublin and we were to go steady for ten months. Her father was a no-nonsense market-gardener from Rush and after a while I started going out to the house for Sunday dinner and tea. I met Connie in the Palladium Ballroom in Rush on Easter Sunday and I asked her out, soon dating regularly. We would go to the pictures but I would always have to go to the pub afterwards for I still felt I would not get to sleep without a drink, something that lasted for years. Connie was a very sensible type and though we kissed and cuddled, that was as far as it went—she made it clear she would not go to bed with me until we got married. Indeed, in a weak moment in August of that year and after a good few pints, I proposed to her and she promptly accepted it. I realised my mistake instantly and regretted it as she told all her family excitedly that we were getting married. I do not think I ever intended to marry her but she kept at me about setting a day. In July, we went to Butlins holiday camp for a week and through no fault of Connie's it was the worst week of my life. Though loaded with Guinness every night, I did not sleep a wink for the whole week. The loudspeakers would blare at 7:00 AM every morning: "Good Morning, Campers,"—and the infernal tune—"Zippidy-Doo-Da, Zippidy-Day. Oh what a wonderful wonderful day" to my agony riddled head. I finally plucked up the courage to break if off with Connie in February 1964 through a pretext that she would not go to a play with me which, she said, was obscene. It was *Lady Chatterly's Lover* and Tony Forde was playing the part of Mellors. She wrote to me frequently after the break-up saying if I would only give up the drinking we could save enough to get married. "We spent a fortune in Butlins," she added tartly. Gerry read all these letters with glee and often taunted me about them.

Connie got married the following September. Her photo was in the paper and I was delighted. I think she is happy. She has a few children. But I would not have made her happy, I am certain of that. I was too caught up in my own problems to make anybody else happy. She lives near me now and I see her at the bus-stop and say a civil hello—no more.

Finally about Connie—One day I was walking down O'Connell Street holding Connie's hand when who passed by but my father, peering out the window of his car. When I got home, he said waspishly, "You'll end up in a one roomed bed-sit without a penny to your name." I brought Connie to the Christmas party in 1963, got very drunk, and abused her much to the disgust of Lil Roe, an elderly Clerical Assistant. On Christmas Eve, they were all going up to O'Dwyers but I was flat-broke and could not go and I later met Connie and borrowed a pound from her. The night of the Christmas party, I defecated in the bed and my poor mother had to clean up the mess. She put it down to a sick stomach. Jesus, she was innocent. Those episodes were tell-tale signs that I was drinking too much but the penny did not drop until years later.

In 1964 I continued working with Michael Corcoran and was doing well—I got my first increment but it was only nineteen pounds a year. In the spring of that year, I was courting a girl whom I cannot recall now in the back-row of the Ambassador Cinema and as our breathing got heavier, I started to believe in an instant that you had to be conscious of every breath you take to stay alive. This too became an obsession and started to keep me awake at night—I would be afraid to go to sleep, as I believed that my breathing would stop and I would die. This may sound ridiculous but I believed it.

At the end of 1964, I was transferred to Division D, the Property Section and the Higher Executive Officer was Des Doyle, a more severe boss than Michael Corcoran. I had asked for the transfer and lived to regret it as the work was much harder than that of Districts Division. I, frankly, was not able for it and it began to pile up much to Des Doyle's annoyance, when he would continually reprimand me. I got friendly with Michael Corry from Limerick. He was a year older than I was and was an expert on sport, which became irritating after a while. However, I was to go on holidays with him to Ballybunion, Co. Kerry in 1965 when I promptly fell in love again.

Jack Lumsden, Tom Hayes, Dermot O'Brien, Fergus Redmond, Christy Power and Piaras McLoughlin all worked in that section. I was later to get very friendly with Piaras and I got into the habit of borrowing money from him. He was a great nationalist and was a grand nephew of Pádraig Pearse. He was Gaelic-speaking and had a large family who all had brilliant academic careers. Pearse died in 1969, not yet fifty from throat cancer. He was a very heavy smoker but he did not drink at all. He had been private secretary to various Ministers for years including Donagh O'Malley. Piaras often said he was embarrassed by the amount he was being paid. He was Assistant Principal when I got to know him.

In the summer of 1964, my mother's sisters, Katie and Anne came home with Katie's daughter Mary Anne. I was disappointed when it was Joe who was selected by my mother to chaperone Mary Anne. One night at a dance in the Crystal Ballroom and when I was well-jarred I tried, vainly, to impress Mary Anne telling her how I got expelled from school. I was really pathetic. My mother was continually getting worried about the state of my nerves and she confided in her sisters. There was one awful scene when I threw my dinner plate on the tiled floor and it smashed into pieces. After that, my mother pleaded with me to go and see a psychiatrist but I refused believing it would do no good and what would I do then?

In August 1964, Uncle Jimmy died of a heart attack at the age of forty-nine. I went to the funeral and my mother was ashamed to see holes in my shoes in the Church. We all went to Uncle Paddy's after the funeral and when Bill was dispensing the drink he said to my father, "Do you mind if I offer Georgie a drink?", to which my father replied, "I'd prefer if he'd wait until he was twenty-one."

In that period of 1964, I would usually go to the Hut in Phibsboro and have a few pints with Joe Doherty; not too many though, if funds were scarce. In June 1964, I went to the Fleadh Cheoil in Clones with Dan McSwiney, Des Sweeney, Gerry Lonergan and their girlfriends. I got so drunk, Dan would not let me sleep in the tent. When they were asleep, I climbed into the front section of Dan's van and puked over his cardigan. The second night I fell into an open sewer and got so filthy, I had to wash the dirt from me under a pump. I spent the whole weekend avoiding my father who was also at the Fleadh in case he would see the state I was in. I came home from the Fleadh early, I was so demoralised.

It was my twenty-first birthday on 22 September 1964 and my mother gave me sardines and toast in honour of the occasion. Myself, Tony and Arthur went to the Castle Hotel where you could get a mixed grill for ten shillings. Compared to the scale of today's celebrations of twenty-firsts, mine was fairly perfunctory. We finished off the evening in Madigans of Earl Street. I was twenty-one and was a total nervous wreck, which showed, in my ashen appearance, which magnified my worries.

It was in 1965 that I developed my worst obsession so far. I began to obsess about the nature of existence for no apparent reason. How do you prove you exist, how do you prove what happened took place at all? This really wrecked my head and I prayed that the previous obsessions would return. You always wanted the obsession you did not currently have. But I was ruled by this new obsession because it was so intangible and the insomnia went hand in hand with it, which continued with greater ferocity. My work began to suffer and I began to hide files, which was discovered by Des Doyle when I went on holidays in the summer of 1965, though I got my annual increment.

By this time I was Branch Secretary of the Union and I took it intensely seriously. A big disappointment that year was not getting elected on the National Executive. I became an accomplished orator at the AGMs of the Union, but made a nuisance of myself by speaking on all the motions. Though, at first, I was very nervous at the microphone, I soon got used to it. Round about that time, a photograph appeared of me in the Union magazine with the caption "Unaccustomed as I am" to great hilarity amongst the members. I was later to be co-opted on to the National Executive Committee when Michael Magner, who had a huge intellect and did not suffer fools gladly, was General Secretary with an allowance of £400 a year. He was very eloquent and was anti-Church and anti-Fianna Fáil which endeared him further to me. When he got promoted to the Revenue Commissioners in 1968, I applied for the job and got second to Dan Murphy who is still General Secretary but at a very high civil servant rank, compared to Micheal. Michael was to die in 1978 at the early age of thirty-eight. He was a huge loss to me as a friend. He left a young wife, Aiveen and two infants.

I had become very friendly with Michael Corry and we would go to Madigans on a Friday night and meet Dan McSwiney, Arthur, Des Sweeney and Tony Forde. It was great crack in the pub, famous for its pints, but no women were allowed. It was a man's bar and everybody was an expert on every sport, Mick being very impressive with his detailed knowledge which impressed Dan, also a great sports fan. The love of Dan's life was the Bohemian's Football Club. Michael had a great capacity for drink but he did not have the problem with it that I had.

In July 1965, I arranged to meet Michael in Ballybunion, the seaside resort in Co. Kerry. Mick was going there with his girlfriend, Kathleen whom he was to marry in 1967. So I made my way alone with a two-man tent, which I borrowed from Arthur and I first hitched to Limerick and called to Mick's mother who was taken by surprise as she presumed, wrongly, that Mick was going to Ballybunion with me and not his girlfriend. I got very ill in Limerick—something I ate and hitched at first to Listowel where I had to get two handles of brushes and nails as I had lost the original pegs in Limerick somewhere. I finally reached Ballybunion and pitched my tent just above the beach and I met Mick, Kathleen, and her friend Brigid Morrissey, whom I became interested in. We would drink our fill and then go dancing and I latched on to Brigid but I later was to learn from Mick that she was not impressed with me at all. She said I was too serious. I had started to drink whiskey and red lemonade by then to help me sleep. One night the tent blew away and I was left without accommodation. I went into Mick's hotel and slept on the floor, which I did for the rest of the fortnight, sneaking out at seven in the morning. When I returned to Dublin, I made a date with Brigid and spend the remains of my money on a curry meal. I do not think that I have seen her since. Brigid is now married and has a large family. In 1965, too, I went to the Fleadh Cheoil in Thurles with Dan McSwiney et al but I have not much to report about it, mainly drink and music that I was getting fond of. But as in Clones, I did not run into my father who had gone there with Eugene McGlynn, a fiddle player from Co. Roscommon. They were great friends, Eugene calling to our house frequently—he was a Garda in College Green.

The obsession about existence continued all that year. It was not a philosophical think as perceived by Descartes—*Cogito Ergo*

Sum—It was sheer neurosis which dominated my thinking for the whole of that year. In fact, normal thinking was not possible for me and I found it hard to apply myself to my work. I spent Christmas day in Arthur Shortt's house in Glasnevin. Arthur was a friend of Fergus and my heart burned to see Fergus but I did not have the nerve to call on him. The old fear of rejection stopped me.

So the year 1966 dawned. It was to be a momentous year generally with the fiftieth anniversary of the Rising, the World Cup and personally, I met the woman who was to become my wife. Piaras McLoughlin was in charge of the Government committee organising the celebrations, which proved very successful. A new beer called Celebration came out to mark the occasion, which would blow the head off you, and it became very popular. The air of expectation in Dublin on Easter Sunday morning was palpable as we marched with Sinn Féin to the Republican plot in Glasnevin cemetery and I was rapt listening to the stirring speeches about the sellout by De Valera. We went down to the Brian Boru which was nearby, full of patriotic fervour.

It was in 1966 that Rosemarie got married—she had gone to England with her boyfriend Seamus Mulready, a communist and a nephew of Ned Stapleton's wife. My father did not approve of the relationship and when Rosemarie came home from England to tell me she had got married in a registry office, I knew my father would be appalled. He did not even know Rosemarie's whereabouts at the time and was sick with worry about it so I decided not to tell him about the marriage, for a while anyway. But Gerry burst into the house one evening announcing, "Rosemarie is home," having seen her in town.

I had no choice but to tell my father and mother and to say they were shocked would be an understatement. My father drank steadily that night as a response to this news. The idea that his daughter would get married in a registry office was something he could not cope with. I have never seen him so shaken.

Seamus came to meet my parents soon after and they put on

a civil front. But the marriage did not last and my mother was pleased some years later when Rosemarie got a divorce, thus freeing her to get married, if she so wished, in the Catholic Church.

Michael Corry and I decided we would go to the World Cup quarter-finals that summer and I joined a savings club in the office. The quarter finals were to be played in Liverpool and Manchester in July 1966. We flew to Blackpool and as I was wiped out of it by lack of sleep there was no hope for me of enjoying myself. I had developed the habit of sabotaging the chance of happiness but not deliberately. The first match was in Liverpool and Brazil and Portugal were playing. There was a carnival atmosphere in the pub before the match with the Brazilian fans decked in flamboyant yellow in noisy form but there was no messing or rancour amongst the fans. We all came to see Pele but we were disappointed as he was kicked out of it by the Portuguese centre-half, spending most of the game limping near the sideline. Eusebio of Portugal was another attraction. He scored four goals against North Korea. We were staying in a hotel in Blackpool and the coach would come to collect us and take us to Liverpool or Manchester but I did not enjoy it much as I was without sleep most of the time and, worse still, had a bad dose of sunburn. Michael Corry did not help matters by slapping me on the back, with me in acute agony. At night after the games, we would drink our fill but I still could not sleep. I returned to Dublin wrecked and watched the World Cup Final, which England won, at home on TV not knowing yet that the following day was to be the most fateful day of my life.

That Saturday, Dan McSwiney collected me from my home and we headed for Kilrush, Co. Clare where the County Flea was being held. With us were John Cullen, Des Sweeney, Des O'Dwyer, all friends of Dan who was doing the driving. As I say, fate beckoned and my life was to change utterly for the better. We were drinking in Mrs. Crotty's, the famous concertina players' pub, and listening to the music which was flying, though it was only one o'clock. I saw two women coming in and said, in Irish, "Let those two charming angels in so that they can have a drink." We got talking. One was Kathleen O'Brien from Passage West, Co. Cork and her friend Enda Collins. Enda was voluptuous and sexy; Kathleen was thin and small with an impish grin. I soon fancied Kathleen, the woman who was to become my wife and we spent the whole day with Enda and her. The lads made a great play for Enda, Des O'Dwyer getting off with her as the day went on. I was enthralled with Kathleen and I suppose it was love at first sight—anyway I was smitten. We all spent the day together buying the women drink, the pub agog with music. I would follow Kathleen to the loo and would wait outside for her, as I was apprehensive that anyone would nab her. But she seemed only too willing to stay with me. Why, I do not know as I had poor self-esteem when it came to women. When the pub closed, we discovered that the women had no place to stay. Des and I invited them back to our small tent and the women, believing that we had a mobile home, readily agreed. When they saw the tent, they demurred but we persuaded them to stay. It was certainly crowded in that small tent, only fit for two, but the four of us bunked down. Kathleen and I kissed and cuddled until we fell asleep and though it rained out of the heavens, I did not care. Des O'Dwyer enjoyed himself too. At dawn of the 1st of August 1966, we sat in Dan's van to ward off the cold and the steam rose from our bodies as the sun came though the window. We were heading home that day and I had not the nerve to ask Kathleen for her address, fear of rejection again, but she took the initiative and asked me for my address and she gave me hers. I promised to write and I was to write to her nearly every day for the rest of our courtship. I still have these letters, full of innocent though manipulative passion. I was elated that anybody would take such an interest in me but I think it was reciprocated by Kathleen. I was a very happy man leaving Kilrush, I can tell you, though this did not quell my obsessions, which were still rampant.

A MEMOIR

When I got home to Dublin, I immediately wrote to Kathleen and I was surprised when she responded by return of post. In early September, she invited me down to Cork and I went with Conor Malone who used to be in my class in O'Connells. Kathleen greeted us at her door in a housing estate in Passage West and said, "You can stay if you go to Mass." Everybody had a great welcome for us and we slept in Sonny and Mamie's next door, Kathleen's Uncle and Aunt who were kindness itself. Kathleen came from a family of six, steps of stairs, and I soon got to know them all very well and liked what I saw. I think they liked me too, I hope so anyway. Kathleen's granny, Nan, stayed there too and she could knock out a fair tune on the accordion. I thought to myself if there is a thing called happiness this must be it. We went down to the local pub with her father, a genial affable man with Mamie's voice in our heads: "come home in time for your dinner." I was over the moon on my return to Dublin and vowed I would marry her at once. Within a fortnight, I proposed to her and she said, laughingly, "What's your rush?" I have been with her now for forty years and though the relationship has had its ups and downs, it has worked, with two children, Conor and Fionnuala and now a grandson, Conor's son, Finn who brings great joy to me in my old age.

Not at my prompting, Kathleen gave up her job in Cork City and came to Dublin to live at the end of September 1966. As she was good as an accounts clerk, she had no problem getting work. The sixties were booming by then and Lemass' rising tide, lifting all boats, had taken off. Kathleen got a flat in Summerhill and frankly it was a dump and she soon moved to 108 Amiens Street which while an improvement was not much better. We courted tentatively at first and were intimate though I did not have full sexual intercourse with her until we got married and awkward and shy I was too on the first night. We would hitch down to Cork on weekends and go to the Opera House or the pictures. I continued writing to her every day, pledging undying love, which I meant and I would deliver the letter personally. How Kathleen got to meet my parents is worth telling. She got locked out of her flat one night before Christmas and there was nothing for it but to bring her home to my place. I waited until my parents would be in bed and gently put my key in the lock. I put Kathleen in the "maid's room" and went to bed leaving a note for my mother telling her she had a visitor. It was a Saturday night and the following morning my mother was full of anxiety about my father's reaction. He was still in bed and my mother insisted that Kathleen be out of the house before he got up, but not before she gave Kathleen a hearty breakfast. My parents got very fond of Kathleen and never stopped thanking God for my good fortune. They soon were to treat her as if she was their own daughter. In later years when my father was getting older and my mother was dead, Kathleen would look after him as if indeed she was his daughter. My parents thought I had fallen on my feet and that meeting Kathleen would have a good effect on me. So it had but I continued drinking in the period up to Christmas. Kathleen would go to the pub with me but would only drink a glass of Guinness—she was never a heavy drinker and I did enough for the two of us. She was a big hit with my friends as she had a huge personality and she got on well with their girlfriends too.

One incident to do with drink stands out from that period. Kathleen had arranged that I would spend the night with her in her flat in Amiens Street as her flatmates had gone home for the weekend. I was over the moon but how could I square it with my father who still kept a severe rein on things and always expected us to be home on the last bus. I persuaded him I was invited to a party in Bray and would have to stay with a friend overnight. Though dubious, he relented. It was a Friday night in November 1966 but after work instead of going straight to Kathleen's place, I went drinking in Baggot Street getting quite drunk. The dinner she had prepared was burnt to a cinder and when I arrived about ten o'clock, she was heartbroken. While waiting for me she wrote a long letter, clearly under great stress,

saying I had ruined what was to be the best night of her life. We
had earlier arranged to go to bed together but I had ruined it.
She sobbed all night with me sleeping on the floor. The silence
the following morning was something else and I went home a
chastened man but this incident, bad as it was, did not stop me
drinking. It was the subject of frequent rows between us and
she sometimes would break the relationship off. Much as I was
besotted with her and needed her, I could not imagine a day
without a drink. I needed it, if only a few pints to help me sleep.
Indeed, Dan McSwiney and his friend Barry Cullen, a teacher,
who was to become a mentor of mine, began to think that I was
drinking too much and even mentioned it to Kathleen. Now
Dan liked his few pints but he could handle it and Barry hardly
drank at all. So the clear danger signs were emerging and I am
still amazed that Kathleen did not leave me on that account.

1967 came and what was in store? In January, I was transferred to Districts Division with Paddy Condon as my boss and
Jimmy Geoghegan, a severe, remote man as the Assistant Principal. This new section was a welcome change from Division D
under Des Doyle and I got to love the work, which I could manage quite well. I was assigned a number of counties and worked
as Executive Secretary to John Hamilton Morgan, a senior architect, a Protestant and a gentleman who suffered from chronic
bad health. He was gaunt to an alarming degree and I was to
learn later he suffered from deep depression. I used to write the
letters for him to sign about schools and Garda stations and, if I
say so myself, I became a dab-hand at it. It was John who took
me on my first field-trip visiting Garda Stations in Kildare and
Meath. And for lunch, we would sit on the banks of the canal eating sandwiches and drinking bottles of stout. These were
happy days. I enjoyed John's company and he mine, I think,
but he also appreciated my work. Paddy Condon ensured that I
would not stray too far but he more or less gave me a free hand
as long as I did my job. John was surprised that I was earning such a small wage. Indeed, in 1968, I borrowed £50 from

him when he inherited money. John would go to Doheny and Nesbitts in Baggot Street to drink and he cut a sad and forlorn figure there in later years, gazing fixedly into his whiskey. Andy Halpin worked in the section too and had a great brain He was forever doing crossword puzzles but was very obliging. I got to know him very well in Personnel when I got promoted in 1970 and discovered that he was a gifted music conductor being in charge of church choirs. Frances Heffernan was my typist and how she could read my scrawl is anybody's guess—but she was very obliging and friendly, if on the quiet side.

Jimmy Geoghegan ruled his section with a firm hand but he let us have our head. As long as we did the work, he was content. He seemed to be humourless and taciturn and if you crossed him, you would do so at your peril. I enjoyed the work in that section and did well for the time I was there until I was moved in mid-1968.

At the bottom of the room, Fergus Gilmore worked with Jim Palmer in charge of Parks. Fergus got promoted to Higher Executive Officer that year and also got married, as did Michael Corry. I was at both weddings with Kathleen and was especially flattered to be asked to Fergus's. He had been courting Martha Murray from Blackrock, County Dublin and she worked in the office as well. How they actually started dating was Fergus was driving during a bus strike and saw Martha at a bus-stop so he offered her a lift. He did not ask her for a date there and then but one day in the office she was on his mind and he took the bull by the horn, rushed upstairs, and asked her out. They now have four grown-up children and two grandsons. Fergus was thirty-four when he got married in 1967.

I think the reception was in the Montrose and Paddy McMahon, Con Sheehan and myself got drinking in the bar long after everybody else had gone. Con was a friend of Fergus's too and was resolute, principled man from Co. Cork. He never got married. He inherited a house from his landlady in Morehampton Avenue near Donnybrook, which is now worth a fortune. Well, we were all in humour for more drink at the wedding and Paddy went to order a round and was refused; though well-tanked we were not drunk at all. An argument developed with the barman and polite insults were traded. Paddy was a quiet man but had a steely side to him and I was the argumentative type myself. Before we could be thrown out we decided to leave—on principle as Paddy said—and we went up to Reddins's Pub—now McCloskey's—on Leeson Street and continued to drink until closing time. Kathleen must have been with us too but so caught up was I in shoptalk, I cannot remember. You could listen to Paddy all night. He was involved in theatre and had directed some plays, one of which I saw—*Drama at Inish* by Lennox Robinson— which I enjoyed. I think it was the first play I was ever at and this began a lifelong interest, which I share with Kathleen. All I can recall of Michael Corry's wedding is that I had a row with Kathleen that morning and she said she would not go to it with me. But she did and we had a good day.

My nerves were going from bad to worse by mid-year and I began to get afraid I would die as I had a searing pain in the back of my head all the time. In all the years since 1961 that I had been suffering, I confided in no-one. But in 1967, I was near to breaking-point, though I was not out of touch with reality then—this was to take another two years—but I felt I had to tell Fergus whom I looked up to. I remember crying in the toilet in a pub one night when I was with Fergus but I had not the nerve to tell him. Kathleen must have guessed though because of my frequent tantrums. How she put up with me I do not know but she did, through thick and thin.

It was in 1967 that my sister Anne had to be hospitalised for paranoia—she was only twenty and was to have frequent breakdowns with delusions. My father spent a fortune on private nursing-care for her but to no avail. She suffered for most of her life and died aged forty-nine in 1996. She was to be given electric-shock treatment, which terrified her, and she would ring me begging me to help her. She spent her life in abject despair and even our family's efforts to help her were to prove fruitless. She suffered intense agony with her delusions, paranoia and visions. One night in Cabra Road, I was minding her and when I would turn out the light and she could see her Staff Officer coming into the bedroom window to kill her. Hers was a lousy life and she never had a chance. She is at peace now, I hope, in a better abode than this world had to offer. She left a husband and three children but our family never see them now. You could feel bitter about this but my parents for one did not talk much about it but my mother never stopped praying for Anne and indeed the rest of us. If there is no heaven, my mother must have got a right kick in the face as she did during her relatively short life—three of her family headcases. It is still too depressing to think about it let alone write about it and prudence requires that I only write about my own experience in the matter. Indeed, in writing this memoir, I am conscious of the need not to divulge anything that may cause hurt. So I will just stick to my own story. I owe it to myself to record, if only for my own use, what happened to me and how I recovered after long years of pain. Part of my reason for writing this is to bring hope to those who may be suffering too. After the dark surely the dawn but not always, for there are those who find life so unendurable that they feel they have to take the ultimate step. Though I thought of this option in my darkest days, and they were yet to come, I never seriously considered the ultimate step. So I guess I was one of the lucky ones though in 1967, I thought I had reached the end of my rope. It was not until 1969 that the weight of unremitting pain became unendurable. There was to be one more obsession so awful that I finally cracked with no hope of coming out the other side. But I will write of this climax when I reach 1969, the year man first walked on the moon, the most significant year in my young life. I was twenty-six, my life still ahead of me, and Kathleen's too; she was still with me at that time. My parents called her a warrior and she was truly. We shared the same interests, theatre, books, traditional music and politics and this must have kept us together. She did not like the movies and rarely went with me.

I first got to know Tommy Peoples in 1967—he was to become a renowned traditional fiddle player and he had then just come to Dublin, having been born in Co. Donegal. He was from a strong republican background. I first saw him in O'Donoghues ballad-pub in Baggott Street. The ballads and the traditional music were taking off then with the Dubliners playing there too. John Kelly from Clare and Hughie McCormack, my father's friends played there regularly too, as did another fiddle player, Joe Ryan. The music would soar to the ceiling and we would drink as if there was no tomorrow. Paddy Donoghue and his wife Maureen were the owners of the pub and they ran a tight ship ensuring that no-one got out of hand in the bedlam. The pub was to become a regular haunt of mine and Tommy Peoples would play with the older men who presided over the proceedings with a firm hand and would not let any newcomer lose the run of himself. In fact, an argument developed one night between Tommy and John Kelly about a perceived breach of protocol on Tommy's part, and heated words were exchanged. John minded his patch with great tenacity.

To my surprise, I met Tommy in the porter's lobby in the OPW the following day. I had not known he worked there—in fact, he had just started as a porter a few days earlier. We soon became bosom and boozing friends and our common interest in traditional music was a bond between us. He knew my father and had met him in St. Mary's Club in Church Street, where my father played with Paddy White, John Egan and Tom Mulligan, every Wednesday. My father also played in the Piper's club in Thomas Street on Saturdays and he enjoyed the quiet atmosphere in the clubs. He did not like pubs and would not play for money—most of the musicians were being paid a pound or two by then. The only time my father played formally was in the Oireachtas competitions but as he was so shy and nervous he never won a prize. He preferred to play by the fire at home on Sunday evenings—it was his only form of relaxation he would say.

Tommy and I got into the habit of borrowing money from each other and we would pay it back on alternate pay days. One Saturday in June, we headed off to the county Fleadh in Mount-bellew, Co. Galway and this was to be my first serious brush with the law—mainly due to drink. There were Tommy Peoples, Joey Walsh, Kathleen and myself and we set out resolutely for the town not knowing what was in store. Tommy was full of devilment and at Rochfortbridge, we saw a garage with a Union Jack flying over it and Tommy, being a fierce Republican, took umbrage. He climbed up on the roof, took down the Union Jack and burned it in triumph. We were chased for a few miles by the garage owner who was in a rage and went to a telephone to call the police. But we made good our escape. We were exuberant if not wild and had scant regard for authority or anybody else for that matter. We arrived in Mountbellew, which was in the heart of the country at about five in the evening. We found accommodation, did our ablutions, and set out for the evening in high and expectant glee. We ensconced in the back yard of a pub and the crack was mighty. To our delight, we found a shed full of bottles of drink and began to help ourselves, free of charge. As luck would have it, the owner did not notice. The music was still going at one in the morning when the Gardaí raided the pub and we were about to be thrown out when a row developed between Tommy and the Sergeant. When Tommy threw a kick at the Sergeant, he was promptly arrested. Like myself, Tommy could not abide authority and the mere sight of a uniform was provocation itself. Tommy was brought to the station and we followed. Joey Walshe, Kathleen and myself, and a crowd began to gather outside the station, I was outraged at events and had a great sense of injustice and began knocking at the station door demanding that Tommy be released. After all, we had only been enjoying ourselves in the pub. I shouted, "You may kill men in Cork or Dublin (referring to incidents there where men died in custody) but you won't kill me." Whereupon the station door was opened and I was grabbed by the collar and taken in. The sergeant proceeded to beat me up and indeed cracked my ribs, which later necessitated treatment, but this did not subdue me. I continued my angry tirade and was put into a cell, which stank with filth. Meanwhile Tommy was released without charge and tried to comfort Kathleen who was distraught. She kept a vigil outside the station door until I was released at about five in the morning, a new day breaking but hardly the harbinger of hope, which it usually is. Before I was released, I was charged on my own surety of disorderly behaviour while drunk and asked to sign the warrant. I demurred but it was only after the sergeant said I would be locked up in Limerick Jail did I agree to sign the document. That night I made one more fatal mistake; I told the Sergeant that I was a Civil Servant in the OPW, believing this would get me lighter treatment which it did not and this was to have serious repercussions for me when I returned to the office after my holidays. I was a chastened man when I left the station that morning and was met by Kathleen. The following day I was afraid I was being watched by the guards but I did not at that time realise the full implications of the night.

Kathleen and I hitched to Galway on the Monday and before I went Tommy begged me to go to the Station and apologise to the Gardaí and they might drop the summons. But I had a stubborn streak in me and I refused, as I was outraged by the fact that I had been beaten up so badly when I had not threatened violence myself. Tommy who apologised was never charged but I did not hold that against him. We hitched to Cork and during our stay I met up with Donie McGrath, a quintessential Cork man, and told him my story. It was only then that the full implications of the incident in Mountbellew hit home. Donie said it was a very serious matter for me and that I could be sacked.

When I got back to the office I summoned up the courage to tell Fergus. But I let the matter sit expecting the actual summons in the post not realising that the document I had signed that night in the station was in fact the actual summons. One Friday night I was taken in by the Gardaí in Store Street for a harmless misdemeanour after a few drinks and would have been arrested but for the intervention of Dermot "Beefy" Farrell from my schooldays who was serving in that station. I was released without charge and went to Kathleen's place to spend the night. She was now sharing a house in Melrose Avenue, Fairview which was clean and spacious and was to live there until we got married in 1970. Without any sense of foreboding, I arrived at my home in Cabra Road on the Saturday afternoon to be greeted by my father, his face white with anger. The Gardaí had been up to the house that morning from Mountjoy with a warrant for my arrest for my non-appearance in Mountbellew court a few days earlier. I was aghast, taken completely by surprise. My father insisted that I go down to Mountjoy Garda Station at once and, fearing the worst, I walked the half mile in anxiety and trepidation. I explained myself as best I could to the sergeant-in-charge and he kindly outlined the seriousness of my situation. His instructions were to arrest me forthwith and drive me to Mountbellew. Like a pathetic child I pleaded with him and he eventually relented if I assured him I would attend the next sitting of the court in early September 1967.

Needless to say my father could not contain his fury. He would accept it if you shot a policeman or a judge for political reasons but a common charge of being drunk and disorderly was more that he could stomach. He promptly ordered me out of the house telling me never to return. Whereupon, I decamped to Kathleen's who was not impressed either. My cousin, Bill, was furious with me too and, in no uncertain terms, he fumed at me for bringing shame to the family. In an incident in 1963, I was also thrown out of the house in November by my father for merely using the F-word and spent a night in McSwiney's, two nights with Paddy McMahon and a week in a flat on the North Circular Road. At Bill's intervention my father allowed me to return home, a chastened young man. I was very bitter about this for years and all my father said was, "I had no choice." But he had, I felt. To throw his son out on a bitterly cold night was a cruel thing to do for what was a harmless utterance. But now the Mountbellew incident seemed far worse and it was indeed. I was beset with worry about the forthcoming courtcase whose full implications I did not appreciate until later. When I told Fergus and then Paddy Condon they were sympathetic but very concerned for me. Fergus got me a local solicitor with difficulty and wrote out a statement for me. Paddy said if I had only told him sooner he could have squared the summons as he had political connections. Meanwhile, Bill negotiated for me to get back to the house to be greeted by my silent father. He was appalled by the incident and felt rightly that I had brought shame on the family. I arranged to go to the Mounbellew court with Tony Forde and Derek Kenny, a friend of Arthur's, who worked in an insurance company. Derek would only drink Red Breast Whiskey. We set out on the road at about seven as dawn broke that fateful September morning; Derek was the driver and an erratic one that, as he had poor eyesight. I was met by my solicitor who surprised me at the outset by saying everybody locally had thought I had killed somebody in a road accident and that was why he was so reluctant to take my case. He said to plead guilty and I would be all right; I would probably get off with a caution. We waited all day for my case to be called, listening with awe to all the other cases which were mostly about local squabbles.

When my case was called at about 4:00 PM, I was put in the witness box and was immediately questioned by the Garda Superintendent who gave me a grilling in a very gruff manner. Previously the Sergeant had given evidence and confirmed to my solicitor that I had not been violent, just verbal abuse. The Superintendent said to me, "Are you not one of those Dublin gurriers who come to Fleadh Cheoils just to make trouble?" Though nervous I immediately replied, "In fact, no, I am not— my father is a traditional fiddle player of some note so I reckon the music is in my blood!"

With that the judge peered down at me over his glasses, "I hope this class of behaviour is not in the blood." I got off lightly with the Probation Act and the judge suggested I put some money in the poor box, which I promptly did. We were relieved I can tell you and set out for home but first of all stopping for a few drinks in the town.

But this was not the end of it by half. The following week, there was a headline in the Connaught Tribune—Fiddler's son has it in the blood—and my father was not impressed I can tell you. After the case the local Sergeant phoned a Superintendent Farrell in Dublin Castle and told him what happened. He was obliged to do so in the case of civil servants who got into trouble. The Superintendent rang his brother Con Farrell who was a Commissioner in the Office of Public Works, a kind decent man but who could not tolerate excessive drinking and who was on the point of sacking me. But he rang my Principal Officer, Jack Walshe, who was also kind and was a patron of mine who told Con Farrell that I was a great worker. They agreed that I should be left off with a stern warning.

So I was called up to see Mr. Farrell who really let me have it but much to my relief he said dismissal would not be warranted. I was shaking so badly that he said, "Now, don't go off drinking, like a good man. However, if there is a repeat, you will be finished. I will have no choice but to sack you." I thanked him profusely and left his office. I was to have one more breach of the law in 1975 again where drink was involved but it really was a hilarious incident based on a misunderstanding. I refused to pay my busfare on some principle and a Garda Sergeant arrested me and I spent the night in Rathmines Garda Station to appear in court the following morning. I got off with a fine and it taught me a lesson. I even went for a drink with the busman who had given evidence against me. I said, "Let me buy you a drink, no hard feelings." Unlike Mountbellew the case did not appear in the papers.

Tony Forde got married in October 1967 to Noranne Garvey from Caherciveen Co. Kerry, a sister of Sean Garvey, the traditional singer. Tony had joined the Civil Service, the Department of Health, the year I did but then moved to computers in the Department of Finance. He was over-ambitious. All I can remember about the wedding is that Tony's father congratulated the bride on her good taste.

I started to go to University College Dublin from October and studied English, Irish, Latin and Economics in first year. I was never disappointed I did not go to college by day like Joe, as I would have cracked up if I had. UCD was then in Earlsfort Terrace and the theatres were thronged every night with rapt students; there was a great buzz about the place with Garret Fitzgerald being by far the most popular lecturer. He taught Economics, which I hated, and he would stay on well into the evening giving grinds to students. He was really enthusiastic but it was hard to follow him at times because of his garbled speech. However, he was kind and considerate and I remember him with great affection.

Before college we would go to the Department of Lands dining club on Upper Merrion Street and eat a huge fry at subsidised prices; I started to neglect my union activities at that time and Michael Magner constantly teased me about it.

We had Gus Martin, Denis Donoghue and Seamus Deane for English; Seamus Deane was inspirational but appeared always to be at odds with the college authorities. I found Denis Donoghue's lectures tedious and he appeared to me to enjoy the sound of his own voice. I scarcely missed a lecture all that winter but did not study very hard. I found Latin difficult—I had forgotten most of my school Latin by then and could never master Economics. I enjoyed Irish with Professor O h-Ailin in charge. He was a brother of John Allen who later became Chairman of the OPW. I would also go to O'Dwyers of Leeson Street after lectures most nights, as I had not kicked this habit before going home to sleep. The ferocity of my obsessions had abated somewhat by the year's end but I still had a persistent fear of not sleeping. Still I struggled on to 1968. What was in store for me as the old year gave way to the new. I went to a dress-dance with Kathleen in December 1967 with Fergus and Martha at the table with the statutory sharing of chocolates and the obligatory taking of photographs. I still have the photograph of Kathleen and myself—she was so thin that Des Sweeney nicknamed her Twiggy after the famous model. I did not like what I saw and to this day I do not like looking at my photograph.

Towards the end of 1967, I started going out to Fergus's house on Saturdays in Churchtown at his invitation. He had a huge garden, which he was knocking into shape and needed my help. I was only too glad to oblige. Kathleen would come out later and Martha would cook a big fry for the four of us. We would go to the Bottle Tower, the local pub, for a few pints and Kathleen and I would then head home. I enjoyed those evenings, though the grouting and lifting of stone flags was hard work.

One weekend in the spring of 1968, Tommy Peoples, Joey Walshe and I decided to go to a Fleadh in Oldcastle, Co. Meath after a drinking session in O'Donoghues. Tommy demurred slightly as he had no fiddle and I said I would get one from my father. So we all headed up to Cabra Road where my father, grinning wryly, said, "Well, we can't have a fiddle player without a fiddle." His injunction as we left —"Make sure you take good care of the fiddle"—rang in my ears and this was to be on my mind for the whole weekend.

We arrived in Oldcastle on the Saturday evening, the Fleadh at its height and as we were a bit short of funds there was nothing for it but to sleep in a haybarn that night which we did after a mighty session. I was keeping a close eye on Tommy all evening as I was anxious about my father's fiddle and the lads knew this. We settled down for the night, our sleep interrupted by midges and fleas and our legs were in knots. The following morning we were stretching our legs and shaking hay out of our hair beside the car when Tommy took a fiddle out of the boot of the car and began to smash it off the ground as if a mad frenzy had engulfed him. The more frantic, I got the more Tommy smashed the fiddle—I did not know what had got into him. The lads were aware of my anguish. "What will my father say?" I groaned. This went on for about ten minutes, the lads laughing heartily. Then after about what seemed an eternity, Tommy reached into the boot of the car and took out a fiddle in pristine condition. "Is this what you are looking for?" he asked, grinning widely. It was indeed my father's fiddle and I was so grateful, almost in tears. I almost kissed Tommy. "We were only having the crack," he said, "we were winding you up." All that Sunday, I kept a wary eye on Tommy as he played. There was only one small mishap, a string broke and the following day Tommy bought one in Walton's music shop. When I meet Tommy now, which is rarely, we always talk about the incident and have a good laugh.

Shortly after that Tommy left the OPW and joined the Gardaí, an unlikely vocation for somebody with a boyishly wild streak in him and a carefree spirit of adventure. He later got married and his fame has spread countrywide and he regularly plays with his daughter Siobhan in gigs around the country. Tommy has not had a drink in over twenty years. But I often think of those crazy days in O'Donoghues when we would head off to a Flea at the drop of a hat and especially the incident in Oldcastle so long ago.

The exams were coming up in May 1968 but before that, I had to sit the Civil Service five-year Irish written test, which was then mandatory. I had been Treasurer of the OPW canteen in 1967/68 and the stipend of £80 was paid at that time. I cashed the cheque after the Irish Exam and Tim Dalton, Tony Forde, Tadhg Tansley, the latter two worked in the Department of Health. Tim, years later, was appointed Secretary General of the Department of Justice and was to become an expert on Northern affairs. So we all headed off to Stepaside for the afternoon, the £80 wad of notes in my back pocket to play pitch-and-putt. We were in great form and after the game we went to a pub and drank solidly the whole evening. Tim was a great mimic and regaled us with imitations of DeValera, Churchill and Lemass. He liked a drink and still does but unlike me he can handle it.

The day was spoiled a little as Tony got into bad form about not getting the job of Private Secretary to the Minister, which Tadhg had just got. Still it was a gay buoyant day and we just about made the last bus into town. I was ambitious but not as ambitious as Tony. We all sat the Administrative Officer exam a week later. This was for honours university graduates but there was a confined competition for serving civil servants and those going to college had a reasonable chance of getting the written exam which I did but there was an interview later which I failed abjectly. I spluttered and mumbled right through it. So I was not surprised with the result. In fact I never succeeded at an interview in all of my forty years in the service.

At the end of May, I sat the first Arts' examination and was feeling very seedy at the bus-stop the first morning because of the perennial lack of sleep. I did very well in Irish, English and Economics, which surprised me, as I had not studied much throughout the year. I failed Latin, which I expected, but I did so well in the other three subjects, I only had to repeat Latin, which I got in September. Fergus ribbed me about failing the first time but I was not so touchy that I could not shake it off.

In July that year, John Morgan allowed Kathleen and me to use his caravan in Ardmore, Co Waterford for a two-week holiday. But the owner of the site nearly evicted us when we let it slip that we were not married. But we held our ground and remained for the fortnight, which we enjoyed, though I was still drinking heavily. John Morgan also gave the use of the caravan to Fergus and Martha and Fergus was to slag me as I had such knowledge of the sleeping arrangements in the small but comfortable caravan. I had drawn him a plan of the layout.

1968 was the year of the failed Dubjec Czech revolution, which the Russians crushed ruthlessly. Paddy Condon could not suppress his glee that, all along, he was right about Russian communism and was not surprised at their action. Paddy was very Catholic; right wing in everything and a devoted supporter of Fianna Fáil, which he never tried to hide—though civil servants were forbidden to belong to a political party, even the one in power. The student revolts in Paris took place that year as well and I was very vocal in my support of them, much to Paddy's chagrin. I was very left-wing then and even joined the Housing marches that year in support of better housing provision. It was brought back to the Office that I had been seen marching to Mountjoy prison to secure the release of an activist, Denis Dennehy who was on hunger-strike there. I never regretted my involvement in this campaign and housing became a huge issue in the general election of 1969. As a result the vast housing-estates in Tallaght, Ballymun and Clondalkin were built but the social consequences of such huge conurbations without adequate recreational facilities were to prove disastrous.

Joe Fahey who became an intimate friend of mine, and still is, joined District's Division that year. I loved his dry laconic wit and put-down sense of humour. He had a good bass voice and was a member of a ballad group for years. He had consummate flair with a pen and settled in under Paddy Condon very quickly. His wife, Connie, who we got to know as well as Joe, died from cancer a few years ago. She had been a Montessori teacher and they had three children. Paddy and I introduced Joe to O'Dwyers pub in Leeson Street but sometimes we would go to O'Neill's of Merrion Row and Doheny and Nesbitt's in Baggot Street which was Joe's watering hole when he was working in the Valuation Office in Ely Place. Joe was a convivial talker and always kept the company rapt in attention unlike me and I envied Joe for this. Joe was as good a listener as I was a bad one but I have now learned the importance of listening. I now know the right to talk implies the right to listen.

I went to work with Fergus who asked for me in June 1968 and he proved inspirational as a boss. There were huge arrears in Dublin Districts when we arrived in that Section and under Fergus' great capacity for hard work and his hands-on guidance we cleared them in a few weeks. Fergus was an effective teacher and his constant supply of work to me ensured I was kept on my toes but he was careful not to overstretch me. We worked with two Senior Architects, John Morgan and Austin Meldon, who had offices on either side of our room with hatches in each wall through which we would put the files. Even an insurmountable task or it seemed to me to be insurmountable would readily be dealt with by Fergus in jig-time. He was a great man for doing business on the phone but he had great facility with a pen when the situation demanded it. Jointly we would keep on top of the work every day with Fergus waiting impatiently for the next batch of files. He had a number of catch-phrases which he used with abandon and which began to amuse me. In other sections he worked in he did himself out of a job within weeks of his arrival. He could master any subject he applied himself to and on that account worked in many Divisions where he was adored by his staff. He may have seemed a bit eccentric but he as on top of everything he did. He hated humbug and did not think much of the Union though he was a member. I remember he hurt me badly when he said I was only a committee member for the sake of self-advancement. This was untrue and I had the courage to tell him so at the risk of losing that friendship. Jimmy Geoghegan was the Assistant Principal and Jack Walsh the Principal, both of whom depended on Fergus as he had a stupendous work-rate in a notoriously difficult Section. I was glad to serve him and I owe my promotion to Higher Executive Officer to Fergus whose leadership inspired great loyalty. But when push came to shove he reciprocated by speaking on my behalf at the 1970 promotion conference. By that time promotion prospects for executive officers in the OPW had improved dramatically through an interdepartmental promotion scheme. As a result when I had gained the requisite seven years' service in 1970, there were only a few executive officers senior to me. But I am certain that I would not have got promoted when I did without Fergus' trenchant advocacy despite what was to happen to me in 1969.

My brother, Joe, got married in August 1968 to Mary

O'Connor from County Tipperary, a friendly no-nonsense woman with a good heart. Joe had set up business on his own following his graduation as a chemist in 1964. Relations between Joe and me had not been good for years but Joe broke the ice just before the wedding by asking me to be best man, which I agreed to readily. My parents were pleased, I know that. I prepared for my duties with diligence, especially my speech which I rehearsed like a demon. I did not want to let Joe down or the family either. The morning of the wedding was spoiled but the day, as a whole was not, by Rosemarie's non-arrival for the ceremony. My parents were stoical and they were determined to have good time and they did. I got a bit emotional making my best man's speech which otherwise went off well and I did not get too maudlin. I did not get too drunk either or spoil the day in any way. My father played the fiddle; Uncle Paddy and Auntie Katie, Bill and Breege and Mary's family were there too. A great day was had by all and we all repaired to Cabra Road for a party, which went on until the early hours. Joe thanked me profoundly for my efforts.

1968 was the year when Michael Magner resigned as General Secretary of the Union and when the vacancy was advertised, I applied but came runner-up with Tony Forde getting third place. I was not disappointed, for I realised I did not have what it took to be General Secretary of a large union with demanding members. I am more convinced of that now but I think Tony was disappointed. But the Chairman of the interview board called me aside to say that they needed us both on the executive committee all the more. By that time I was chairman of the branch committee, distinguishing myself by ruling Paddy Condon out-of-order at the first meeting which reduced Paddy to indignant huffing and puffing for the rest of the evening.

1969 was the year when my whole world collapsed around me. My fraught nervous system disintegrated completely brought on mainly by another obsession, which came in to my vulnerable consciousness as a freak of nature. I was in my second year at college doing nothing but attending lectures, as we did not an exam at the end of the term in June. Drinking by then had become a habit but was not as bad as previous years and I opened a bank account in the Spring and began saving with a view to putting a deposit on a house for Kathleen and myself – intending to get married in 1970.

I had had the same dog since 1964, Smulk, an adorable Wicklow collie, and we were up beside the dog-pond. It was a June evening and the sun was casting a shaft of warm light through the trees and I had my economics book on my lap pretending to study. I was relaxed and totally unprepared for what was next to happen. For no reason, the thought occurred to me that if the earth were flat we would be unaware of night and day as we normally are. Like that morning long ago in Westwick, an obsession got hold of me with tremendous ferocity. What about tomorrow? Where is yesterday? I tried to imagine the passage of time as a burning fuse but I could not find a metaphor to encapsulate the nature of time. Panic set in and the obsession stayed with me all through June and July. Sleep was out of the question. I went down to Cork with Kathleen but there was no soothing balm. I knew I was cracking up, so intense was the pain and drink was no good—it just did not work anymore. Reluctantly, I went to the Galway Races with Joe Fahey, Joe Boland, a work colleague, though my mind was in chaos. There was no hope now, I thought, as we reached Galway and booked into our digs. I did not have a wink of sleep that first night though I had had a few jars. "What can I do?" I said. The following evening, I was pacing up and down the dwarf wall facing the Skeffington Hotel in Eyre Square. I suddenly vowed that no matter what I would do I would see a psychiatrist on my return for Dublin. I did not care any more that treatment might render me unconscious for a year. I would go for any treatment prescribed. Though I was eligible for promotion the following year, I did not care what happened. I made up my mind to go home on the Thursday fully determined to see a Doctor. When I got the train the following evening, I was with Joe Boland, a nice understanding fellow and I regaled him with stories of my escapades. I never laughed as much, the relief was not as palpable as if my mental problems were solved but I knew it was a start. To decide to see a psychiatrist after eight years of terrible suffering was a giant step for me—just as walking on the moon was for mankind a week earlier. I had watched it on TV.

When I got to Kathleen's place, where I stayed the night, I told her of my intentions. She was delighted but the disintegration of my mind had yet to come. Certainly the vitality of my psyche had been eroded over the years but insanity had not yet set in. This, I think, happened the following day when I started to go into the dangerous, nether regions of the mind leading to a gradual but total insanity. I slept well in Kathleen's place on the Thursday night and woke up the following morning refreshed. I had decided on my strategy by then. The only person I completely trusted to help me through this crisis was Fergus, but he would not be home until five in the evening and I would then ring him and tell him I wanted to go into hospital. I was fully certain of that and I decided to kill time by going into town and, on the spur of the moment, I decided to buy a pair of shoes which I lost on the way to the Cabra Road. I did not mind one bit even though they were expensive. I started to walk home but got an enormous panic attack with my heart pounding, fearing I would die at any minute. I started to run saying if I make it home, I will be all right. It was still only one o'clock and it was four hours before I could ring Fergus. I knew at that point that I was cracking up—this was it, something I had feared would happen to me for years. I went out to the back-lane, the lane of my boyhood, then full of innocence, and I had a golf ball in my hand. I kept banging the ball against the ground and then retrieving it for an hour or two. "This is it, this is it," I kept repeating as I bounced the ball. At five o'clock, I went to ring Fergus but there was no answer—he might have gone away for the August Weekend, I thought, and I began to panic and went home with the intention of trying later. My father had just arrived by then and I told him. "I'm having a nervous breakdown," I said, fully in touch with reality at that point. I told him I wanted to see a Doctor and needed to go into hospital and said not to worry, "I have the money." This was important to me after years of profligacy. First, I had a bath, washing myself over and over and when I was finished, my father said he would first bring me to the Mater hospital to get tablets to settle my nerves. I went with him as he drove in his ford Anglia he bought from Willie Sheridan a few years earlier, Willie assuring him, "It's a bargain, with low mileage." We were met by a Doctor who listened carefully to what we had to say and said, "I'm afraid there's nothing I can do for him here—he needs to see a psychiatrist. Go up to St. Brendan's." I was quite calm, though this was the greatest crisis I had ever experienced. My father drove me up to St. Brendan's—poor, poor man—and we were met by a nurse who called a Doctor. They were very few on duty that evening because of the holiday and I explained everything to him but as I appeared perfectly normal and not at all deranged or mad, he said it was not necessary to admit me to hospital. He made an appointment for me to see the Registrar of the hospital the Tuesday after the bank holiday to fully assess me. That assured me and my father and we went home.

The following day, my parents were due to go to Leitrim for their annual builders' holidays and my father wanted to bring me because he did not wish to leave me on my own in the city because of what had happened. At that point, my fear of my father had evaporated and I wanted him to be proud of me. My parents' annual holidays were largely chasing dreams as only Uncle Paddy was left now in Leitrim. I was full of nostalgia as we travelled for I had not had a holiday in Leitrim since 1960. I was very happy and a little weepy—a bad sign though I had no way of knowing this—I thought it was just sentiment. We stopped for a drink along the way and in order to emulate my father I ordered a bottle of stout as he had done.

I cried in Uncle Paddy's with a strange sort of joy on both Saturday and Sunday and my father explained to him, "Georgie had a bit of turn." The first signs of elation or euphoria were setting in but I was not aware of the significance of this. I was deliriously happy and all my obsessions had vanished. This was life as it should be, I was well again. On the Monday, my father drove to Dromod Station to catch the train for Dublin, a Station I knew from my childhood with its happy memories. On arriving in Cabra Road, I told Mary, Joe's wife that I was having a party to celebrate getting well and I bought bottles of stout from the pub next door. Mary was concerned for she knew that this feeling of well-being was a bad sign but I was happy as larry and did not care. For the first time in my life, I was free of worry and I planned to enjoy it. The following day I was to meet the Doctor and I went down to St. Brendan's but I was told the appointment was not until the afternoon. This was when I made a near-fatal mistake. I went up to St. Peter's Church and got confession. I broke down weeping in a paroxism of relief. I believed that it was my conscience that had been bothering me all these years and now that I had confessed all my sins, all was well again. So I returned to St. Brendan's with a light heart convinced that there was nothing wrong with me any longer. When I met the Doctor I told him that I did not want to be hospitalised after all and that I was better and he was confused, looking at the notes from my visit the previous Friday. So he let me go, for what else could the poor man do. I could not wait to tell my parents the good news when they came home later that day and if they were disappointed, I was too happy to notice. Never had I been so happy.

I met Fergus that night in the Hut and had only a few drinks. I did not feel the need for drink anymore. Nothing out of the ordinary happened that night, as I was not yet out of touch with reality. Wednesday was uneventful too but I was still in high-good humour but my mind was beginning to work overtime and my conversation was rapid-fire. I had a bit of a disagreement with Mick Higgins who was to be the photographer at my wedding. I was inclined to be impatient and testy but the alarm bells did not start to ring at that point with my parents or Fergus.

But on Thursday, my behaviour became erratic. In the morning, I was going to work as pillion passenger on Gerry's motorbike but I told him he was driving dangerously and I got off the bike in protest and finished the journey on foot. I was used to buying the Irish Times from a vendor outside the OPW and refused to do so that morning, much to his surprise. The same day, I gave £50 to a work-colleague when we started talking about prayer and how he prayed fervently when his daughter was sick. I broke down crying saying I believed in prayer too and gave him the £50 without him asking for it. In the afternoon, I got into an argument over somebody who rang saying he was in charge of something or other and I retorted, "I wouldn't put you in charge of a dustbin," thinking I was being very smart. That evening, I went to O'Neill's pub in Merrion Row and got hysterical because the barman said he loved Jackie Kennedy. I was not drunk and I went up to O'Dwyers of Leeson Street and, having had a pint, for no reason, I lay on the floor refusing to budge for Billy Twyford.

I had forgotten that I was expected home to Cabra Road where Kathleen had been asked to tea. I then got it in to my head to go out to RTE and deliver a diatribe against Gay Byrne who I decided was an immoral person. But thankfully, I did not. I went home at about 9:00 PM and my parents and Kathleen were very distressed about my late arrival. I turned off the television and declared, "I have great news for you all. I am a genius." This must have had a terrible effect on those I loved and they me. I then went on to say, "You were wondering where I was tonight, like Christ in the Bible. I was about my father's business."—a reference to Christ in the temple with the elders. I was clearly making comparisons to Christ and my parents knew it but felt powerless. I went to bed blissfully unaware of the havoc I had caused. Though my mind was still racing, I was elated by the fact that I was a genius and that my father would be proud of me. I was now surely his son.

The following morning I sat at my desk for a few minutes and immediately got up with sudden urge to go to Jack Walshe's room. This was the most momentous moment in my whole life, I thought. Jack greeted me in his normal friendly way and I said urgently, "You will have to sack the Chairman." "Why?" asked Jack. "Because he passed over a friend of mine for promotion." I broke down crying and Jack came over to me and put his arms around me and asked, "Were you drinking last night?" Repelled, I said, "Is that all you can say? This is an important day for Justice, the Office and Ireland."

Jack called Fergus, who knew immediately something was up and they tried to talk me into going into hospital. But I refused saying I was perfectly sane. "Would you not do it for me?" Fergus pleaded. He was now crying. The mad are the last people to know that they are mad and I had gone over the brink. Fergus said, "I'd like you to meet a priest friend of mine on Monday, would you do that?" I said, "I would. He will probably say I am saint."

I took a half-day that Friday afternoon feeling that I was on the verge of doing something great. I rang Tony and told him to put his personal house in order because I became convinced in an instant that he was a sinner. Following the cleansing of my soul in confession, I was now determined to punish sinners. I was now as pure as the driven snow and my mission was to cure the world of its ills. The son of a carpenter, like Jesus. I did not think I was Jesus but I believed that I was as saintly as him. I went home to be greeted by my parents who were extremely distressed. They had been on to Fergus to try and get me into hospital, as what had happened the night before made it clear to them that I needed urgent hospitalisation. What Fergus told them about that morning must have appalled them. I was literally out of control and each minute the delusions where getting worse. But I was as happy as larry, the black sheep at last was coming into his own. The years of pain had been worth it all. I had surely earned my joy.

On Saturday, I went out to Fergus for the usual gardening but I first called into Madigans of Earl Street and ordered a pint. When Mick Madigan, the owner, served the pint, I said, "I am not paying for that for you are an honest man as you sacked dishonest men." What could poor Mick do but accept the situation, confused as he must have been. The afternoon at Fergus' was routine grouting and cutting of grass but at tea, Kathleen started to sob, to me inexplicably. Fergus and I later went to the Bottle Tower and I got very agitated at what seemed like an inordinate delay in being served. Fergus watched with concern.

My parents were shocked to see me when I got home as they fully expected that Fergus would have, somehow or another, got me into hospital. I woke up on the Sunday with anticipation of even greater things. It was only about 7:00 AM and I headed up to the park with the dog. For no reason I started jumping over ditches and fences believing that I was fit enough to play for Dublin. I began to stop teenage boys and ask them if they were at Mass that morning and if they were they would be picked for the Dublin team.

Then the situation took a dangerous turn. I got it in to my head that all car-drivers were dangerous and going too fast so I proceeded to step out in front of passing cars forcing them to come to a sudden halt. I was delighted. I ran home to my father to tell him the good news. He was now my true friend and I had no secrets from him. When he heard about the incident with the cars, he rang Dr. O'Donnell who called to the house to see me. I was flattered but it was clear to him that I was stone-mad. He agreed with my father that there was nothing for it but sign me into hospital.

I was sitting in the kitchen when two burly men came in— they were nurses from St. Brendan's—and they were going to take me there by force, if necessary. "Would you not go?" my father pleaded. "There is nothing wrong with me," I insisted. "I know that," my father said, "they just want to take your name off the books." This reassured me and I came out of the house to be greeted by a line of Gardaí and an ambulance. Gerry, my brother, was there. On that fateful August day in 1969, I was perfectly sane—only me and my father knew it—it was our secret. In the ambulance it occurred to me that I would have to demonstrate to the patients in the Gorman how well I was, having been so sick. But how will I best do this, I wondered. I yapped gaily to the ambulance driver about affairs of state, after all wasn't I the working man's friend? I was greeted at reception and thought if I showed that I could conquer flame and water, I would surely prove to the patients how sane I was and encourage them to get well too. So I asked the nurse on duty for matches and paper—he politely refused. Gerry had left at some point and I was brought into a ward and put lying on a bed, with two nurses watching my every move. So I decided to play a game with them; I would pretend to get out of the bed and they would sit on me—joining in the fun, I thought. This continued for a good while. I had no intention of escaping as I had a mission here. The nurses took off my clothes and put me in pyjamas and I lay on the bed continuing with my game. Then they turned me over and stuck a needle in my backside and started counting. I began to get drowsy but I could still hear the count, 70, 80, 90, 100, 110, 120, 130, 140, 150—getting sleepy now, can't keep awake, sleep, sleep, and sleep 160, 170, 180. I could hear 180 and thought this must be my IQ. I was never happier and I then fell into a deep sleep. It was the 5th August 1969 and I would be twenty-six years old in September.

I awoke from my deep deep sleep at about seven o'clock in the morning and looked around me. Patients were in beds along the barred windows through which the morning light was shafting—they all appeared asleep. I got up, refreshed, and walked out the door and up along the tiled corridor where I was met by what I presumed was a male nurse. He stopped me and asked, "Where are you off to?" I said "I have to go to work, I have a lot of important business to attend to." But he said "You have an appointment with the Doctor at ten o'clock," which baffled me. I said I did not need to see a Doctor, as I was perfectly well. "Well," he said, "you will have to have breakfast anyway—you'll have a fry, won't you?" "OK" I said "I'll have breakfast but I must go then." The dining room was at the end of the corridor and I sat down looking around me. There were only a few men there at that early hour. I ate my breakfast and pondered on all that had happened to me the day before. I was still very elated and excited about the new life ahead of me, free of worry and obsession.

I tried the outside door but it was locked and went back to the ward and proceeded to gaze out the window and watched the gulls scavenging for food and thought this is the life. The windows were barred and the floor of the ward was pristine polished. No harm in waiting for the Doctor, I thought, though I must then be on my way, as Fergus would be worried. The clock on the wall seemed to be at a standstill as I waited and I looked at the patients still asleep in their beds. Poor wretches, I thought. I got talking to an elderly man in the bed beside me—he said he was a boxer and had fought amateur for Ireland. A nurse came to help him and said, "Jim, you've ruined your sheets again—what a mess."

The old man asked me if I had a cigarette and I said, "I don't smoke." "Stay off them then, they are a curse." He had the rasping voice and cough of the inveterate smoker. The nurse came back with fresh sheets, and changed his bed, and they got a basin of soapy water and proceeded to wash the old man as if he were a window. I thanked God for my happy lot and felt overcome by an overwhelming pity for the man. The other patients, about six in all, were by now getting up. "Where's the loo?" I asked Jim. "Just down the corridor," he said. I was bursting to go but try as I might I could not. I could not relax which is a vital requisite. There were half doors on the wc's and patients were shaving. I was handed a single max-smile blade by a nurse, who was supervising and I shaved, enjoying the feel of the soft soapy suds.

"The Doctor will see you now," a nurse said at about ten o'clock. "Does he have a name?" I asked with just a hint of impatience. "Yes, Dr. Meehan" he said. The nurse brought me up to the Doctor's room and knocked. "Come in, Mr. Rowley" a middle-aged grey-haired man said—"Have a seat, I am Dr. Meehan." "Hello Doctor," I said.

"And how are you?" he asked. "I am fine, couldn't be better. But I have to go to work. Got important business to attend to." "What's your hurry?" he asked, "We have to keep you here for a few days—just for observation. Yours is an unusual case."

I felt flattered and reassured by this remark.

"I am at your disposal, Doctor. I'll do my best to be of assistance to you and your staff. I am anxious to be of service," I said.

He then surprised me by reciting well-known proverbs and asked me to explain them which I did. "They're easy Doctor," I said. "That's all for now, George, I will be seeing you—I am just anxious to monitor your progress." "Ok, Doc. I am at your disposal," I repeated grandly. I went back to the ward and said to myself—there is no harm in co-operating with these good people. I was still convinced that there was nothing wrong with me and that my father knew this too.

Lunch was at one and the hands of the clock seemed to crawl like a snail. "The food is like slop here," Jim said, "It would poison you." Rattle of trolley, rattle of cups, and the nurse almost perfunctory—he seemed so heartless as he dispensed the food, which was, indeed, vile but I ate it and drank the lukewarm tea. "Piss", Jim said, "Have you got a smoke?" I waved my hand a little imperiously. "Don't smoke," I said. "Stay off them, they're a curse," Jim said.

I walked up to the end of the corridor and tried the door—locked. I could not leave anyway as I was still in my pyjamas. I looked in at what appeared to be a snooker room—went down to the bottom of the corridor—door locked. "No way out of here," I said. Sat on my bed trying to while the time away until tea, which was at five. The black and white forties films were on the TV and held no interest for me and I again looked at my watch. At 3:00 PM, the nurse came to me with a large tablet on a plate and a glass of water. "What's that?" I asked suspiciously. "It's part of the observation process that Dr. Meehan discussed with you this morning." I did not demur further as I was anxious to co-operate. I tried to lie down to sleep to pass the time but a nurse nudged me, "No sleeping during the day!"

I wondered how my parents were, how proud my father must be, I thought. Tea came on cue, a boiled egg and scones, tea still lukewarm. I tried to go to the loo again, not a drop. Got talking to a young lad in the corridor, he was convinced that he had got his girlfriend pregnant. He was dressed in a fine blue suit. "I am getting out tomorrow," he said. I did not know whether to believe him or not.

Just before I went to bed at 8:00 PM, the sun coming through the window with specks of dust dancing in the rays, a nurse came to me with the same big white tablet. I swallowed it without demur. My mind was still racing, beginning to get obsessed about not being able to urinate and I told the nurse. He assured me I would go when my bladder got full. The other patients were getting ready for bed too and I immediately went to sleep to awake again at 7:00 AM. The same routine as yesterday, a big fry, a tablet. I gazed out the window on to the hospital lawn and longed for home. I saw Dr. Meehan arriving at 10:00 AM but he did not return my enthusiastic wave. I was disappointed. Nothing to do but stare at the walls. Jim was beginning to get me down. Lunch at 1:00 PM, mutton, I hate mutton, plain jelly again lukewarm tea and one Marietta biscuit.

The nurses sat behind a glass panel, impassive, like statues but they watched the movements of all the patients with great diligence. At 4:00 PM, the nurse bellowed "Bath Time". "I don't want a bath," I said but he insisted: "It's always bath time on Tuesdays". We were all marched in to a room with communal showers and told to tog off which I was reluctant to do.

I didn't want anybody looking at me. I was so ashamed of my body. I was particularly ashamed of my small penis but the nurse in a no-nonsense way made sure I had a wash like everybody else so I had no option but to agree. We used a big bar of carbolic soap with the other lads howling with laughter.

Then tea at five, again a boiled egg and watery tea. The routine would kill you, I thought as I got ready for bed but not before I was given a tablet. I tried the loo again but I could not go. I was getting worried.

The following morning after breakfast the nurse said "The Doctor will see you at ten." About time too, I muttered to myself. "You are doing well," Dr Meehan said "but I want to keep you for few more days for further observation."

"OK," I readily agreed, "but will you send a message to my boss, Fergus Gilmore, he will be worried." "Will do," he replied and that was the end of the consultation.

I did not know it at the time but my mother had been down to the Hospital and was met by Dr. Meehan who did not hold out much hope for me. The treatment might or might not work he said shaking his head. This must have distressed my mother but I did not learn of her visit until I was released from hospital. We were allowed out to the grounds under supervision and I just walked around to get the lie of the land. The grounds were spacious and I wondered where the main gates were so I could go home. I was now very homesick like the time a lifetime ago in England. Back to the ward, lunch, tea, tablet, clock motionless. Thursday and Friday came, same routine and I found myself getting drowsy during the day wanting to sleep all the time but the nurse would not let me. Tried the loo again, and could not go. I was in agony now. My racing mind had now slowed up and though I still was convinced I was a genius and as saintly as Jesus, it did not seem to matter to me as much. I did not know it then but the tablets were having their desired effect. This was only explained to me later when I got back to reality. Meanwhile I still thought of playing for Dublin and vowed as soon as I got my clothes back, I would go out to the fields to practise. My vision started to get blurred and I could not concentrate on the newspapers which patients had discarded. So there was no way I could pass the time. On the Saturday, I was allowed out of the ward to go to Mass, which I did and I received too—a great comfort to me it was. I had got my clothes back by then.

On the Sunday, we were given a treat for lunch, chicken and ham, sprouts, peas and loads of gravy with fresh fruit salad and ice-cream. The usual tablet and I sat on my bed counting the cracks on the ceiling. The Sunday visitors started to arrive. I was not disappointed when none arrived for me. There was a middle-aged man down the ward who was crying because his mother had not arrived. He sobbed all afternoon. I was to learn afterwards that his mother had been dead for years.

I had not had a drink for over a week now and frankly I did not miss it. For, somehow, I could sleep now without it—as I said, I was drowsy all the time and eventually put it down to the tablets and another unending day passed. I was not conscious of the nature of time or existence, catalepsy, insomnia or breathing any more which had so obsessed me previously, which nearly destroyed me.

It was 6:00 PM on the Monday. I had had my tea and tablet when the nurse called me and said, "You have a visitor!" I did not want to see anybody as I was so drowsy and could not focus my thoughts at all. I looked up from my bed. It was Fergus smiling broadly in his boyish way. "How are you?" he asked. "OK, but bored out of my mind," I replied. "You'll be better soon," he said. "I'm all right now," I said. He talked about this and that, then silence. He mentioned the troubles in the North, which had just erupted, and though I usually had a passionate interest in Northern affairs, I did not show the remotest interest in the topic. Now Fergus told me afterwards that this was when he re- alised that the tablets were working —indeed they were slowing me up—my mind was not racing anymore. The feelings that I was a genius and a saint were diminishing but I could not wait for Fergus to go, I was all fogged up, battened down so much I could not concentrate.

I know Fergus went up to Cabra Road after his visit to tell my parents that I was responding to treatment and that there was hope for a full recovery, however slow. He had spoken to the nurse before he left who had given him those assurances. But it was to be a long haul. Soon other visitors started to arrive. My parents, the ever-reliable Gerry, Joe Fahey, Joe Boland, Kathleen, Con Sheehan, Tony Forde but I never allowed them to stay too long. Time passed slowly and the monotony was beginning to get me down. I was sent to what was called therapy, which was mind-bogglingly boring, stitching magazines together and getting them ready for posting. It nearly drove me mad it was so tedious. I stopped going after a while.

I had found a way out on to the grounds out a side-door and I would slip out to play ball on my own. I still had a notion that I would play for Dublin but it began to fade as the days went by. Kathleen had been a regular visitor and she would bring me chicken and tomato, which I would eat guiltily, the patients in the ward trying to sleep time and monotony away.

I continued to go to Mass and receive every day though I had not been to confession. The eternal days dragged on and we were soon heading for September, my favourite month. One day after I met Dr. Meehan, I was given an extra tablet. "That is a sure sign you're getting better" the nurse assured me. I had gotten to know the routine by then and I often escaped out to the garden though I no longer practised football.

The feeling of greatness and being a man apart had by now disappeared. I seemed subdued but I had none of my old obsessions now and was still sleeping soundly. I could now go to the loo intermittently. I started to wonder when I would be discharged for I was now aware that I had been signed into hospital, by Gerry most likely. One day I walked through the grounds and wandered out the front gate—nobody stopped me.

I walked down the quays and into town and went into Bewley's on Westmoreland Street and had two cream cakes and coffee. I could have bolted but I did not. Being a sectioned patient, I was prohibited from leaving the hospital so I rushed back and my absence had not been noticed. One day, Joe, my brother, came to visit me and he was very upset at seeing me. "Things haven't been good between us," he said. But he would make it up to me when I got out. The two of us got very emotional. My sisters, Mollie and Noreen, came too. Anne did not, so I figured she was in hospital again and Rosemarie was in Luxembourg at that time. I had been so wrapped up in myself I had not thought of others. I am still to this day very self-absorbed but I am working on this defect.

One day Dr. Meehan told me "We're moving you to a new unit. It is much more salubrious than the one you're in," he said, "you'll have your own room and shower." I was relieved. "But when am going to be discharged?" I asked. "Be patient," he said, "in a week or two, at the most." The new unit was like a luxury hotel compared to 10A where I had been. You could come and go as you pleased as long as you were in time for meals and bed. One day I took my courage in my hands and walked up the familiar Upper Grangegorman, the cottages of the 1940s and 50s and the memories engulfed me. I had decided to visit my mother and she was delighted to see me, though a little apprehensive that I had escaped. It was like old times—we cried a lot and I said I was sorry for the hurt I had caused her. She said it was not my fault. "I never stopped praying for you and Anne," she said. I can still see her now—a frail little doe, in a blue smock flecked with paint. Despite all her troubles she had never lost her gaiety or optimism.

I was uplifted by this visit and I soon got used to calling up to her and she would put on a huge fry for me on each occasion. Now it was the second week in September with no sign of a discharge date and I began to get frantic. Fergus reassured me and Dr. Meehan told me one day "You'll be discharged on Friday. Drop into me at ten in the morning and I will sign the papers." The long ordeal, the endless day would soon be over and, though delighted, I was not elated or out of touch with reality. I thanked all the nurses that morning and went to see Jim in 10A. He was still there but could not remember me. "Have you got a cigarette?" is all he said. I met the young lad who was supposed to have made his girlfriend pregnant. He was still in his new suit. "I am being released tomorrow," he said, his eyes bright with excitement. I do not know when and if he was ever released. He would be in his sixties now. Poor fellow, I thought.

I waited patiently outside the doctor's room. After an hour went by, I began to fret—I sought reassurance from a nurse. He said everything was in order. I was shaking with fear. "What if there is a mistake?" I blubbered. "There's no mistake," the nurse said. At about twelve noon, Dr. Meehan came out of his room and greeted me with a large smile. "Well, this is your big day. You were a model patient," he said, "at first we thought that there was no hope that we'd get you back to sanity." "And I thought I was perfectly ok," I said. "That is how bad you were," he replied.

"There's one thing, Doctor, I have to ask you. Can I drink?" "Yes" he replied, to my relief. "You can have a glass of stout. I have made an appointment for you to see Dr. McKeown next week." "Why not you, Doctor?" I asked. "I am going on a sabbatical," he said. I knew he had restored me to some semblance of sanity and I was grateful. I shook hands with him and never saw him again—he was dead within the year. I walked down to the Quays and up to Madigans of Earl Street and ordered a glass of Guinness, my first drink in six weeks and sat back and took in the scene. Freedom, I thought, is precious. Mick Madigan was not there. I was glad. I did not want to be reminded of that awful Saturday when I was completely out of my mind, awful for me, awful for my parents and friends, especially Fergus.

I vowed I would never be a patient in a mental hospital again except as an outpatient and I never was. I had been nearly six weeks in St. Brendan's and the memory of it has never left me. I found the traffic strange with the noise and the angry horns, as I walked home up to Cabra Road. They were all there to greet me. My parents, Gerry, Joe, my beloved Kathleen and all the girls except Anne and Rosemarie. I was home but little did I know it that this was only the beginning of a long and arduous road to full-recovery, which I only achieved in recent years. The delusions and obsessions were gone but I was a long way off full recovery, a recovery which I delayed by my own hand through excessive drinking, the remedy of which only came for me in the 1980s. Fergus had checked with the Doctor to see when I could go back to work. "Immediately," he said. So I went to work on the Monday full of fear; I bought the Irish Times and when I went in everybody had a great welcome for me.

Tommy Connelly, the Principal Officer in Personnel, rang me and said he hoped I was better. There were plenty of calls and Joe Fahey brought me to coffee where I thought everybody in the canteen was looking at me. I was shaking with fear. Fergus had arranged with the Branch Committee of the Union that I should stand down as chairman of the branch, much to my disappointment. I was supposed to go to the Aran Islands on a Gaeltacht scholarship but that was cancelled too. Again disappointment. Pauline Gilmartin from the Michael Corcoran days was now the typist, familiar ground indeed, which put me at my ease. I still remembered the fifty pounds I was owed but I did not mind as I was flush having had little or no expense while I was in hospital.

I was sleepy all the time and could not concentrate properly. But Fergus eased me back into the job gradually over the next few weeks so that I was not put under any pressure. I do not know what I would have done without him in that fraught period when everything was strange even new to me.

Jack Walsh called to the room with a grin. "I am glad you're back," he said and left again. There was even a get-well message from the Chairman. I am embarrassed to this day about what happened in Jack Walshe's office that morning. Fergus was his old self, working like a demon with flair and in his inimitable way.

I decided on my own not to go back to college for the final year though Fergus said it would be ok if I did. But I had lost my enthusiasm for it. I went home immediately after work and went straight to bed as I was tired all the time—I was on heavy medication. I was on 500 milligrams of Largactyl per day, which was a heavy dose by any standards. I wanted to go to Croke Park for the All-Ireland football final but my father would not let me so I watched it on TV, Kerry winning. I was back to normal, if you could call this normal.

I had my first outpatient appointment on the following Monday so I went up to the Gorman on time and had to endure a long queue until I was called to see Dr. McKeown. He was a blond bespeckled man in his thirties and at the outset I thought it important to tell him all that had lead up to my breakdown. Dr. Meehan had not dealt with this at all when I was a patient in the hospital. Dr. McKeown said I was a manic-depressive with a propensity for mood swings and obsessional thoughts but with medication I could control it. He stressed that it was essential to stay on the medication for the rest of my life which concerned me.

There was a long wait for the medication after I left the prescription at the hatch waiting for my name to be called. I was to continue going for outpatient treatment in St. Brendan's until 1984. After I got my medication I went around to ward 10A to try and recapture the experience of my six weeks there. I spoke to Jim but he did not remember me. I met the young man I referred to earlier in his new suit. "I am getting out tomorrow," he said. Nothing had changed. The highly polished floor, the clock, the nurse on vigil through the glass, appearing immobile; I was glad to get into the air again and I sat on a seat and watched the ducks waddling nonchalantly at ease in their skins. I went home and straight to bed.

Life continued like that until Christmas, with my weekly out-patient visits, the long wait to see Dr. McKeown and the longer wait for the medication which I took every day as prescribed. I was very careful about that. I tried to go to the pictures with Kathleen but I could not relax and was inclined to get a bit pan-icky in the dark. I was watching my drinking and was conscious of Dr. Meehan's injunction of limiting it to a glass of stout but I was not always successful. Neither of my doctors ever questioned my drinking, though I am now convinced that it was a factor in my breakdown. But I assured myself that it was the obsessions, which came first. I was still getting flashes about the nature of time and existence and Fergus rang Dr. McKeown about this who assured him it was part of the recovery process.

Sleeping had been restored completely and I was never to worry about insomnia again. For reassurance I thought of the injection I got the day I arrived in hospital and said, if all comes to all, I can get one again to knock me out.

Christmas came, as did 1970, a new decade and if the last year had been momentous, this too was be a big year for me. I got engaged on April Fool's day, got promoted in July 1970 and got married to Kathleen in November. I had saved enough to put a deposit on a modest house in Beaumount on the northside and this was to be my home for the last thirty-six years although Kathleen is now talking about moving in the autumn of our years. Kathleen must have been heroic to marry somebody after a nervous breakdown. I am not aware that anyone advised her against it and I am grateful for that. I got on very well with all her family and visited Cork frequently. When I got engaged on 1 April, Dana won the Eurovision song contest. We had a few drinks in Mooney's of Phibsboro and went home to a party. Though I enjoyed myself, I went to bed early being overcome by tiredness.

On 24 July 1970, Fergus answered the phone and said I was wanted up in Commissioner Farrell's office. I was full of fear, wondering what was up. This was the man who called me up when I got into trouble in Mountbellew. So naturally, I was on edge when I knocked at the door. He welcomed me but had a stern face. "George," he said, "Is there any reason why I shouldn't sack you?" I nearly collapsed with fear. What had I done? When he saw my reaction he said, "I am only joking." We are promoting you, George, to Higher Executive Officer starting in Personnel on Monday." I could not believe it. I thanked Mr. Farrell profusely, saying I would not let him down and rushed down the stairs to tell Fergus the good news. He laughed heartily—he knew already. Jack Walshe had tipped him off. I did not do much work that day, I can tell you, my desk being clear anyway. I invited all my friends in the office for drinks in O'Dwyers of Leeson Street after work. We had a great night— Kathleen was there too. All had changed utterly in a year but a new crisis was about to envelop me. I started in Personnel on the Monday and my Assistant Principal was Cyril Griffith who was a gentleman and very calm. Even working on his files he would constantly smoke his pipe, the fumes rising to the ceiling of his glass-panelled room. I was again put on the industrial side with a staff of two: Leo Doran and Barbara Mullins. Supervision was a new role for me and at times you would think Leo was the boss when he would decide which tasks he would undertake. Barbara was easier to handle—she was in charge of calculating industrial lump-sums and pensions. I did not like the work from the outset and the week was not out when I developed a severe crisis of confidence. I felt the work was beyond me and within days I thought I would never cope. As the weeks went by I developed an obsession about my apparent lack of ability and could see no way forward. I spoke to Cyril about my lack of confidence and he did his best to assure me that this was normal in the case of a first promotion, especially as I was so young. But this crisis was to continue for the whole time I was in Personnel, which was two years. I decided in a fit of despair to revert to executive officer but some native cunning in me stopped me. But I definitely decided that when I was eligible for Assistant Principal, I would write to Personnel to say I did not wish to be promoted to that grade. But again, when the time came, I did not write to Personnel either. Indeed, I made strong objections to Jack Walsh when I was passed over for Assistant Principal in 1978/79. I suppose, deep down, I was ambitious and would normally not let anybody in the Office do me an injustice.

There were two weddings in the family in 1970. Gerry got married in June, to Peggy Campbell, and I was best man. I was very nervous at the altar, quaking in my shoes. But all went well and we had a great day at the reception in Malahide repairing to Cabra Road for a party afterwards. Then my big day arrived on 28 November 1970. On the night before the wedding Uncle Paddy arrived with Auntie Katie and he gave me ten pounds. My father gave me a hundred pounds—he gave the same amount to each of the family when they got married. I spoiled things somewhat the night before by trying to get the seating arrangements changed. Kathleen and my mother were furious at this last-minute intervention and they stood their ground. Kathleen's parents arrived, as did some of her brothers and sisters. Sonny and Mamie were there as was Uncle Sean and his wife Eileen.

I was very nervous the morning of the wedding. As I waited outside the Church in Fairview, I watched enviously when I saw Des Sweeney and Joe Fahey going into the Fairview Inn at opening time. I was immaculate in my tailor-made suit and Joe was best man. I was nervous at the altar with Kathleen at my side, to be with me for the rest of my life. The reception was in the Marine Hotel in Sutton and just before the meal Bill said to me "Whatever you do, don't get drunk" and I did not.

I still hate looking at my wedding photographs, as I was monstrously overweight. I was nearly fifteen stone, aged twenty-seven, on the most important day of my life. The crack was mighty when Uncle Sean played the fiddle and was joined by my father who was surprised that Joe had put his fiddle in the car. He demurred, at first, when asked to play but then joined in and played all day. All the men there seemed to have taken the Republican side in the civil war; Kathleen's Uncle Maurice in deep conversation with Uncle Paddy, both of whom had been activists in the 1920s. My mother cried her fill, relieved no doubt, that the agony of the previous year was now over. There was one hitch, the bar was closed during the holy-hour and Des Sweeney complained loudly. So we all headed for Cabra Road where we had the best party I was ever at, if I may say so myself. My mother had a four-course meal for everybody though we had eaten at the reception. Joe settled the bill with a cheque, which I had written. It came to one hundred and sixteen pounds less a deposit of ten pounds. The collection at work that Fergus had organised paid for the whole lot.

We were going on our honeymoon by mail-boat and coach to London. This was not doing it on the cheap. Both Kathleen and I did not like flying. When the time came for me to leave, I got very sentimental and told my mother I did not want to go. She quickly retorted "Well, you're not staying here tonight." My mother could be firm when she wanted to be.

Joe drove us the ferry and we barely made it, arriving as the gangplank was about to be pulled up. We immediately decamped to our cabin, with two bunks one over the other. I climbed into Kathleen's bunk and though we had been intimate in the past, I was not a great success at full sexual intercourse for the first time. But as time went by I got the hang of it with Kathleen gently encouraging my efforts. We disembarked at Liverpool and got a coach to London Victoria, stopping along the way for a steak and kidney pie. We spent a week in London, having a few pints of bitter and at night going to shows. I did not drink too much. Work was still on my mind but I tried to forget it. We saw all the sights, which I had last seen in 1961. A lot of water had gone under the bridge since then, I mused. I was wondering what the lads were doing at home and got sentimental. We met Sean Lineen, Mollie's fiancé for a meal out—he was from England and living in London. I like Sean a lot and he was to marry Mollie in 1972. They have four children all grown up now. They have all done very well.

We went to Liverpool by coach for the second week and stayed with Kathleen's cousin Mick, Sonny and Mamie's only child, who had been in England since 1955 and worked in the car industry. We drank a bit but I was glad to get home. Kathleen and I did not have a row during the honeymoon. We stayed with my parents until our house was ready at Easter 1971. Joe and Gerry now had houses of their own so we slept in my old bedroom with the single beds. One night Kathleen and I were in bed together and my mother came in. "Excuse me," she said and promptly exited.

I was fed and watered like a prince when I was in Cabra Road with Kathleen, never wanting to leave. I kept putting off the date when we would move into our own house. My mother and Kathleen were falling over themselves looking after me. I went back to work with trepidation and all the old fears tormented me. We spent Christmas in Cabra Road and I must say I was happy despite the feelings of inferiority about work. This was to last until 1972 when I was transferred back to Districts' Division, the place where I had been more secure.

We moved to Beaumont in April 1971 and as we had good money we were able to afford carpets and all the other furniture. I still remember terrible feelings of low self-esteem when we were laying the mustard-coloured carpets.

PART FOUR

1971–1980

THE NEW YEAR DAWNED FOR THE ROWLEY family with the news that Joe's wife, Mary was expecting their first child—a first grandchild for the Rowley dynasty. Their son Paul was born in February 1971 and I went to see the new arrival and held him in my arms. I was nearly as excited as Joe was. His business was going well and he had bought a house in Sutton and by now we had patched up our differences. I had been at fault too when relations between us had got strained. But I was not one to keep up a grudge and Joe was not either. They had two more children, Brian and Claire, who when she got older became the dead-spit of my mother, just like Aunt Katie in America. It was uncanny how she looked.

My drinking was to get heavy in 1971 and when I went on holidays to the Aran Islands with Kathleen that summer I was a total mess. I was to completely forget the doctor's limit of a glass of stout. So soused was I with tranquillisers and drink, I spent most of that holiday in bed. I have a photograph of myself in Galway that year and I, frankly, looked grotesque.

Back at work, I went on a course in Landsdowne House in

Ballsbridge for Higher Executive Officers. I got so depressed by my seeming lack of ability, I left the course early and went straight to the pub. 1972 was worse for drinking and I drank every day that year including Good Friday. I spent my summer holidays in Passage West that year and spent the whole fortnight drinking in the Club bar in Glenbrook—this time gin and tonic which I had got to like. I think my drinking crossed the invisible line between heavy drinking and alcoholism that summer and there was no apparent reason for it. I had transferred to Districts Division that year with Jimmy Geoghegan as Assistant Principal, stern as ever. I went to Galway races for the August weekend and thought back on 1969 and its calamitous aftermath. I went with Joe Fahey but I did not enjoy myself for I knew that I was a physical mess. I was revolted at my appearance. I went to the wedding of Kathleen's cousin in October and disgraced myself mainly because somebody said I was old enough to be Uncle Sean's brother. We went to Kathleen's brother's wedding that year too but I do not remember much of the detail.

Anne and Mollie both got married in August 1972 and Anne was so high at her wedding she made a long convoluted speech. They got married within a week of each other and the bedlam in the house the morning of each wedding was overpowering. I got drunk in an early-house both mornings and felt so awful that I though I would collapse.

Noreen graduated that year and my father got dressed up for the occasion and my mother had a new outfit with a hat. And I was driven to despair again at University College Dublin when a porter thought I was Noreen's father. I was vain enough to be worried about my deteriorating and ageing appearance but I did not seem to have it in me to do anything about it. As a child, I was so good-looking that women would say to my mother that I should be in the pictures. Yes, I was vain and terribly self-absorbed. I was still taking the same dose of medicine and Kathleen worried at night in case I miscounted the number of tablets I had taken. How she put up with me, I do not know. I had settled into the work in Districts Division and was in charge of a number of counties with Mary Kelly and Christine Devitt—working closely with the Architects, which I enjoyed. But I started to neglect the work by 1973 and was now getting into trouble through excessive drinking. I was inclined to blame the medication for my travails but deep-down I knew drink was the basic problem. I was aware drink was the core of my difficulties but could not see a day without it.

We went to Dingle in July and then on to Dunquin and I had good news in May 1973, I learned Kathleen was pregnant and I was overjoyed. She had a bad pregnancy, getting sick all the time and bleeding a lot. We had to have it confirmed a few times that she was still pregnant. My mother got sick that year from the cancer that would eventually kill her in 1977 and had a kidney removed. When she was in hospital, Anne cut her wrists in an effort to get attention. She was still being hospitalised frequently.

Anne had a baby son in February 1973; the phone call came to Broughan's the house next-door and I went in to answer it. It was Alex, Anne's husband; the baby was premature Alex said and I replied "You can say that again." I always had a sharp tongue. My father was at Mass that Sunday morning and my mother left it to me to break the news to him. He did not mind and I think he was glad that Anne was married. Anne was to have two more children, Jennifer, and Jonathan, who was a bit of a surprise after ten years. In later years, I would bring Anne and Jonathan for lunch on pay-days and give her money. Jonathan used to drive me demented jumping up and down all the time and Anne got me down too with her moaning how impoverished she was. Anne was to say "George loves meeting me" but in fact the two of them drove me to distraction.

The strength and forbearance of my mother when she was ill was extraordinary. One day we were in Bewley's after I had brought her to St. Luke's for a check-up. However, my mind was elsewhere as I had to ring the Coombe Maternity Hospital to see if Kathleen was still pregnant after I had left in a sample a few days earlier. My mother, always thinking of her children, knew it was on my mind and said "Go and make your phone call." And when I brought back the good news to my mother, she was overjoyed. Anne was always on her mind even up to her last few weeks when she was nearly unconscious in St. Mary's Hospital in the Phoenix Park where she was to die.

It was coming to the end of 1973 and Kathleen did not look pregnant at all. She was due in January 1974. At Christmas, Kathleen came into the Office and Jimmy Geoghegan said "Go home with your wife" when I asked him down to the canteen for a drink. Jimmy was a great family man and very serious—he seemed to be devoid of humour. On 31 December 1973, we were staying in Cabra Road and the baby was not due for another three weeks when during the night Kathleen thought the baby was coming. So we got a taxi to the Coombe but she was discharged the following day. Then on the morning of 3 January 1974, her waters broke and this time it was for real. Joe Fahey drove us in and the baby was born at about 9:00 AM, three weeks premature. I was over the moon when I held my son, Conor, in my arms for the first time. This was a life-fulfilling dream and I went to Lowe's pub with Joe for a celebratory drink but not too many. I must have been elated, even on the dangerous side, as I got a Mass of thanksgiving said and I went to confession and communion. I sent telegrams to Uncle Paddy and to Kathleen's grandmother, Nan. Paddy, later, was to say "there was never a Conor in the Rowley family."

Conor was to remain in hospital for three weeks, a period fraught with anxiety for Kathleen and me. I never prayed as much – he was in an incubator a lot of the time and we monitored his progress, worried that we would never get him home. I made all sorts of promises that I would, at least, cut down on the drink and I did, only having bottles of stout, albeit large ones, in Downeys pub on the Cabra Road, telling everyone about the birth of my son.

Conor finally came home on the 24th January 1974 and I vowed that I would be the best father ever, not repeating the mistakes, as I saw them, of my own father. It is for Conor to say if I was a good father but I can honestly say I did my best, as I now admit my own father did. Unlike my father, I did not believe in corporal punishment at all and I can only remember resorting to it once or twice. On the funny side, when Conor and Kathleen were still in the Coombe, I went shopping with my mother for clothes for Conor in Clerys. "Nothing but the best would do for my first born," I said but my mother, being more experienced and thrifty, opted for middle-priced clothes, nappies and not top-of-the-range as I had said I wanted. We often laughed about it afterwards. We kept Conor in our bedroom for a good while and I would often get out of bed during the night to see if he was still breathing. Conor is now thirty-three and has turned out well—he is now married with a son of his own to whom he is devoted. I hope I taught him a few things along the way about rearing a child.

When Conor was christened, we had a great party in the house afterwards and Joe Boland distinguished himself by falling into a bath full of baby-clothes. I took a week off work after Conor was born and though I was still elated, I was afraid to go back in case anything had blown-up in my absence. The year Conor was born was in part a turning point in my drinking pattern. We got a photograph with Conor at Easter and I was worried about how fat I looked and vowed to do something about it. So I started to drink infrequently and for the next few years, I was off it for long periods.

I went to West Kerry in August on my own with Kathleen going to Cork with Conor. I stayed in Krugers and only drank in the evenings. In September, I was awarded a Gaeltacht scholarship and the whole family went to Carraroe in County Galway. I stayed for a fortnight with Kathleen and Conor staying for a week. Conor was the centre of attention in the digs and I felt happy and proud. One significant thing happened that glorious fortnight, I started writing songs *as Gaeilge* and, though I am still embarrassed by my first effort, it was a start on what I have been doing since. My father had that talent too and I was soon churning out lyrics to well-known pop songs. I can put a lyric to any tune with equal facility in Irish or English. Sometimes combining the two for the sake of a rhyme. I cannot resist a rhyme, which has the effect, I think, of reducing my poetry to a jingle. But after that hesitant start in Carraroe in 1974, I was on my way to being creative. But I was not to write my first short-story until 1985 when I was fully off the drink for a year.

I kept to my pledge of only drinking periodically and I became towards the end of 1974 and the beginning of 1975 a periodic alcoholic. I would be off it for long periods and for no apparent reason I would go back on it again but only for a short period. I was determined to get fit and improve my appearance and I joined a gym in early 1975, the Grafton Health Studio of which I was a member for years until it closed in the eighties. I gradually began to lose weight with exercise and diet and began to look well in photographs taken in that period but I would still break out from time to time.

In 1974 a few work-cases had blown up because of neglect on my part and I got into trouble with Jack Walshe who was now a Commissioner. He had proven he was kind and considerate when I got ill and had like Fergus became my mentor. But this did not stop him writing, on a file which I had badly handled, "Allowing for all the difficulties in this case and there were many, it is hard to believe it could be worse handled"—a harsh judgement indeed. Fergus' protective mantle was no longer there and I was cruelly exposed. But as Jack was to say to me in 1979, when he promoted me to Assistant Principal and I was apologising for past lapses, "You had bosses too."

When I would go into a pub in that period the lads would ask, "Are you on or off it?" and I would usually be off it. In 1975, Kathleen got pregnant again, which we had not planned and the baby was due in November. This was an easier pregnancy than

Conor's was and both Kathleen and I were very excited by the prospect of a play-mate for Conor who was now walking and chatting with gibberish.

I went to Gweedore in June on a Gaeltacht scholarship and the high point for me was singing my own composition on Raidió na Gaeltachta to the air of *Forty Shades of Green* which went down well. I had gone to Gweedore via Ballinamore and spent the weekend there mainly to make amends for an indiscretion in 1973, which was received without grace by the person involved. I had a few pints with Michael Crossan, Uncle Jimmy's old friend in John Joe McGirl's. I was in great form and though slightly elated I was not dangerously so.

On the Monday, I got the bus to Donegal town and hitched the rest of the way. We had a great time with songs and music every night in the famous Hudie Beg's pub in Bunbeg with the O'Maonaighs playing most nights. I sang a bit too and was somewhat in demand because of my performance on the radio. We sat around a bonfire on Midsummer's night, a million stars in the sky and I felt so content I could count them all.

Kathleen wrote to me reporting Conor's progress almost on a daily basis. After Gweedore, we went to Dunquin for our annual holidays and my drinking was limited to a few pints of Smithwicks when we had put Conor to bed in Kruger's, owned by the genial Padraig O'Neill. I really enjoyed that holiday with the sun shining brightly every day and we would walk with Conor in the buggy as far as Comenoll, a lovely beach with the frantic surf cascading with abandon on the shore. I read a lot on that holiday, mostly John Steinbeck and some Liam O'Flaherty. I soon had nearly all Steinbeck's works read. West Kerry is my favourite place in Ireland and it was really idyllic that summer. Peggy, Padraig O'Neill's mother, would sweep the floor at closing time urging us to go to bed but her pleadings fell on deaf ears. Padraig was not a good accounts' manager and when it came to settling our bill it was ridiculously low and I wrote the cheque with a flourish.

We had the new baby to look forward to in November and both of us were very excited hoping for a girl. Fionnuala was born on 4 November 1975 and again like the occasion of Conor's birth, I was over the moon. While Kathleen was in hospital her sister, Esther, came to mind Conor and I took the opportunity to go for a drink with Tony Forde in Sinnott's of South King Street, then owned by Eugene Wilson, brother of the Minister, John Wilson.

Tony and I were having a serious but genial chat when who burst in but John Fitzpatrick, a friend of Joe Fahey's. John was showing the signs of a long day on the booze and we were not in humour of him. Eventually, I had no choice but to bring him home after a generally enjoyable evening with Tony had been cut short. I was to awaken during the night and went downstairs to see John in his red underpants sitting in front of the convector heater, his pot-belly looking monstrous. I persuaded John to go to bed and when he got up, he could not wait to go to the local pub for a cure and ring his girlfriend of long standing—though I do not think that they ever got married. John was normally good company. He worked in the Post Office and was a great raconteur but, on that occasion, he was a nuisance, which I know I often was.

I had started going to Club Chonnradh na Gaeilge with Noreen at that time and my Irish was becoming very good. I would sing some of my own compositions in Irish, which were well received. Noreen then asked me to do a translation of *Here, There and Everywhere*, a Beatles hit, for a Slogadh competition in which her class were performing. Noreen had got her Higher Diploma and was teaching in Ballymun where she was to work for nearly thirty years. But I was at a disadvantage with her request as I did not know the song. So I bought the record, playing it over and over again until I got the hang of it. I had the pleasure of seeing the translation of the song performed for Slogadh and though it did not win a prize, I was as pleased as any playwright would be on a good first night.

I was only drinking occasionally towards the end of 1975 but when I did, it was inclined to be a ferocious binge. Colm Jackson, the doyen of O'Dwyers of Leeson Street, was dying of cancer in Baggot Street Hospital that December and I went to visit him. I drank for oblivion that night and when I went to work the following day, the withdrawal was so bad when an architect came to talk to me I could see his lips moving but could not comprehend what he was saying. It got so bad that he seemed to be moving all the time—he was just standing there in a normal fashion—it was clearly a bad case of the DTs and I had to get to the pub immediately after work to settle my shattered nerves. These binges, occasional as they were, set in train a series of panic-attacks, which frightened the hell out of me.

At this stage I could not control my drinking once I had begun and had got into the habit of lunch-hour drinking, surely a bad sign. But some of the lads were doing it too so I thought, wrongly, that it was all right. We would drink about five or six pints at lunchtime and go back to work and think nothing of it. I was still going to St. Brendan's as an outpatient, taking my usual dose of medicine and never once was I questioned about my drinking.

In 1976, my mother got a stroke caused by a brain tumour, which was inoperable, and she was confined to a wheelchair. She still had the same gay heart and impish humour. My father was convinced until the day she died that she would somehow get better but she eventually had to be hospitalised in St. Mary's, a dreary forsaken place where she ended her days strapped to her bed; it was a clear sign she was getting worse when her bed was gradually moved towards the wall of the ward.

My father who had been working for Bill for a few years in his workshop and got a full non-contributory pension in 1976, despite the fact that he had considerable savings. I was advised by a Principal Officer in the Department of Social Welfare that if my father could show that he was dependent on his savings by frequent withdrawals from his bank, he would get a full pension.

He did what I advised and the day my mother got her stroke was the day that my father got news of the pension. My father was convinced that the stroke was a sign from the Gods that he had done something improper, that he was not entitled to. A year earlier my brothers and sisters began the practice of putting money regularly into his account, which he did not notice for a good while. He said to me when he discovered it, "That was a nice surprise I got today."

In April 1976, I went to see Rosemarie in Luxembourg where she was working for the European Parliament. It was my first time on the continent and having flown to Brussels I took a train to Luxembourg where I spent a week but I drank a lot and got an enormous panic-attack at the airport on my way home, so much so, that I thought I would not be able to board the plane. When I got home to tell my parents how I got on, I was in such a state of panic I could barely speak.

Things were changing in the job, changes that would affect my future for the next fifteen years. The schools end of Districts Division was being amalgamated with the New Schools' Division and it was decided that I would go with the schools end of things. I was pleased with my new boss, John Berkery, who was friendly and easygoing and let me have my head. I was to work with the schools Architects who appeared to be standoffish and too protective of their role. But I soon got on well though. I was not on close terms with the architects as I had been with John Morgan—no lazy days on the banks of the grand canal, I'm afraid. I had a few staff who were very capable and working only with schools was a relief. It was non-schools work, which had got me into trouble in 1973/74. I soon got on top of the job and was regarded as an expert on it.

I went on a Gaeltacht scholarship to Ballyferriter, Co. Kerry in June 1976 but I was very depressed right through and I did not enjoy it at all. In July, Kathleen, myself and our two small children went to Ballyferriter and stayed in the Dun an Óir Hotel for a fortnight. We were handicapped without a car, which was essential with the children. Kathleen said it was the worst holiday she had ever had, being confined with the children in the hotel most of the time because the weather was so bad. My old insomnia obsession had returned and I was then drinking at lunch-hour to help me sleep but I could not. It was a miserable fortnight and we were both glad to get home.

1977 was a bad year; it was the year my mother died and Fionnuala was put in plaster as one of her hips was out of joint. She was a sad spectacle with her legs kept apart by a stick all the time and a nappy was out of the question so there was always a mess when she went to the toilet. Because of this, we did not go on holidays that year and anyway my mother was dying. She died on 11 November 1977 and in the weeks before her death we would visit her every day—she, though unconscious, puffing the cigarettes Gerry would put in her mouth.

I got a call in the office that my mother was on the brink of death; poor soul, she was unconscious, breathing her last. I had had a few drinks at lunch-hour and I broke down sobbing at her bedside as she lay dying. As her life ebbed away, I thought of her firm religious convictions, which she steadfastly clung to all her life despite her difficulties when three of us had got sick. It must have broken her heart but she never lost her deeply-rooted faith. She was indeed heroic and if there is any such thing as a saint, she surely was one. She died at six in the evening, her whole family with her. She was sixty-six years old. Recalling the photograph of her with Auntie Kitty taken in 1960, I was to write in 1980:

> *Lonely, pitied, with hapless aid*
> *By those who would shortly braid*
> *Hands clasped in fear of death's ecstasy*
> *With crucifix and rosary.*

The funeral-mass was said in her beloved St. Peter's church where she had gone to mass and communion every day and where she did her Monday-night novenas and nine first Fridays regularly. We buried her in Glasnevin where she is now resting with my father who died in 1983. My father never got over her death. "What will I do now?" was his constant refrain to Noreen who was the last one to leave Cabra Road and who got married in 1978.

Noreen had been doing a line with Paul Bates for a number of years, and when my mother heard this she enquired, "What does he do?" "He's an executive officer in the civil service," Noreen replied. "Hold on to him then," was my mother's cryptic reply. Noreen and Paul broke up once when they were courting and when the line was on again, you could see the happy light in Noreen's eye, smiling as a child would on her birthday.

We went on holidays to Ballyheigue, Co. Kerry, a seaside town, in the summer of 1978. It rained all the time, so I had an excuse to drink and I soon got to know the barman who allowed me to pull pints for myself. We went to the Merries and we had a good time. The Whitesands Hotel, where we stayed for the fortnight is still there and I often visit it when I am in the area. My nerves were in good shape that year and I was not drinking too much with the exception of the holidays. I returned to work and all was going well. I was still involved with the Union but not with the same fervour.

Noreen and Paul got married in December 1978 in St. Doolock's Church in Kinsealy and, though it was a momentous day for bride and groom, my father was very morose and did not speak a word. He was still in a desolate trauma after my mother's death. Paul was to do very well in the civil service and is at present an Assistant Secretary General, the second-highest rank achievable. Noreen is now a deputy principal and is a very committed teacher. You should see her animated gesticulations when she talks about her job. They have two sons, Eoin and Colm who are very talented at music. Joe's son Paul is a very gifted filmmaker in America and has won numerous prestigious prizes. Mollie's four children all have had brilliant academic careers. If only our parents had lived to see their successes, they would have been very proud. Joe's business has gone from success to success and he is very well off—though you would never think it—he is not pretentious in any way, though he owns a few houses. He is very generous and is committed to our family. Gerry is now a Principal Officer in the civil service—Gerry who never studied at school and is happier on that account. Rosemarie retired from the European Parliament some years ago and is now an established poet and essayist. So we have all done well, despite our humble background. My father's strategy demonstrably worked despite my misgivings about the methods used.

None of my siblings drink much, ok they would have drink at a party or a wedding but none of them have developed a problem with it. So what happened me, why was I the exception? Well, I can hazard a good guess. I was a deeply troubled young man and I drank to kill the pain. The more pain I was in the more I drank. But I also drank because I liked it and I drank too much, too often. I also liked the pub and the company and I was good fun to be with until drink began to take over and eventually I let it dominate my life.

I was still going to the gym and losing weight. By 1978, I was down to about 150 pounds, and the photographs from that period show a man in his thirties looking fit and well. Vanity was the main driving force in this. I had hated looking like an old man, which would drive me to despair. I was in good form in that period only drinking periodically but I could not stay stopped. I only learned to do that in 1984 when I gave drink up completely, principally for the sake of my family, my health and also I wanted to be a writer something that stayed with me since I was a teenager. Indeed when I met Mr. Carey in town in 1964 he asked, "Have you written that book yet?"

I was still writing songs namely about the Dublin team who won the All-Ireland in 1974, 1976 and 1977. I never lost interest in the Dubs, which is still a passion, and I am glad to say Conor, my son, is following suit. We often go to Croke Park together and while I am inclined to lose my head, Conor is silent, just like Uncle Jimmy who would chew grass during a match. I only hope my grandson takes up the baton when he gets older but like with my children, I do not push my views.

January 1979 began with a disappointment work-wise for me—Pat Connolly was promoted to Assistant Principal, though I was senior to him, and Joan Forde was promoted in Parks. I was furious. I went up to Jack Walshe to complain and I almost put him into a corner I was so enraged. He was a bit taken aback with my vehemence and I listed about twenty attributes for an Assistant Principal and asked him if I possessed them. He said I did and I replied then why was I passed over. He said that both Pat and Joan had long experience of the work and the Chairman wanted to keep them in their areas. I was somewhat reassured but I insisted, "Don't let that happen again." "I won't," he re- plied and I believed him. Jack was honest and sincere and was to keep his word. Though I was always insecure about my worth, I could always stand up for my own interests and would not let anyone put one over on me. I had left my bad work perform- ances behind me and was doing very well in Schools. Jack was true to his word and on Valentine's Day 1979 he called me to his office to give me the good news and I did not decline the offer. I had never got around to writing that letter that I was not interested in further promotion. I put it down to natural cun- ning and self-preservation. I was kept in the Schools' Division where I was charge of a large staff and I had no inhibitions as I had when I was promoted to Personnel in 1970. I was familiar with the work by now and the staff who were very loyal to me. I put great store on loyalty. Kathleen was delighted with my news but my father did not like the prefix assistant—neither did Uncle Paddy. Paddy was very proud of us and in his local pub in Edentinny, he would say "Tell them how much you are earning now and what grade you are." Paddy and my father were very close, though theirs was a silent relationship and Paddy treated us as if we were one of his own children. He was very proud but a bit on the vain side. I see him now standing in front of the mirror getting ready for Mass and as he would preen himself with perfume and Brylcream, Katie would dust him down. He would get a taxi to Mass every Sunday and go to John Joe McGirl's after, but first drinking a glass of water before having a drink out of respect for the Holy Communion. He was a devoted DeValera man and a member of the Knights of Columbanus. He had had a sad life with his first wife dying in childbirth and his only daughter drowning in 1942. Getting married to Katie was the making of him and they were like two turtle-doves, even in old age. He died in 1981, and John Joe's son, Liam, was in charge of the funeral arrangements. As the coffin was being placed on two chairs outside the house, Liam asked Bill, Paddy's son "Do you mind if we put a tri-colour on his coffin?" "Certainly not," Bill said, "but no speeches." We gave Paddy a great sendoff and I saw my father merry with drink for the first time at the meal afterwards. Paddy is buried with his parents near Drumshanbo—Bill asked my father if this was ok. I often thought it was strange that he was not buried with his first wife, Mary Kate, in Fenagh. Indeed, it is Auntie Katie who now lies with Paddy in the Rowley plot. May his noble soul rest in peace. He was a great man despite his misfortune. His son, Bill, his grandchildren and now his great-grandchildren are carrying on his name.

The day I was promoted in February 1979 Barry Cullen was taken to the Church, dead at forty-two. Barry was a lifelong friend of Dan McSwiney as well as his brothers Paul and John and had become a good friend of mine, often cautioning me about drink. He was a very cultured man and was a teacher. Though he had had many girlfriends who all turned up at his funeral he never married. He was great man for dancing even as he got older—he was a big hit with the girls and was a gentleman. His brother, John who had been at sea for years went out with Kathleen's sister, Mary, for a while. Mary still talks about him but it was not to be.

Conor and Fionnuala were going to school by this time and

I took a keen interest in their progress, though I was careful not to push them too hard as my father had done with me. I cried at both their Communions and brought my father for a meal each time. The family used to take turns at bringing him out and Kathleen and he got very close. She idolised him and he her but she would gently chide him for his non-stop smoking even in bed. I first bought a car for Kathleen in 1977, second-hand, and she would drive my father home on a Sunday night after dropping into the house for a nightcap, usually a Baileys. My father never became a serious drinker, even as a widower, though he liked a drop of whiskey or a bottle of stout. When my father got older, and on his visits, I could see his whimsical humour and dry wit something that passed over my head when I was a child. He would spend hours playing with my children, who looked forward to his visits, as he would never forget to bring them sweets. But, one Christmas, I lost my temper with him when I was trying to fix up a train I got for Conor. I was getting frustrated at my failure to get it going and when my father tried to help, I turned on him saying something about my childhood. There these outbursts were very infrequent on my part. When my father got ill with prostate cancer, I had the privilege of bathing him and helping him fix up the bottle for his urine. I knew then I loved him and I knew he loved me even once telling me so. I have long since forgiven him for any wrongdoing, as perceived by me, and I hope he forgives me too for my obvious shortcomings. Neither my mother nor father ever thought I drank too much—even my mother would complain that I drank too slowly when I was out with her. I would sip the Guinness but with great resolution.

I went to Majorca with Kathleen and the children in the summer of 1979 and I found the crowded beaches and the high-rise apartments intimidating. It was my first holiday in the sun and though I spent a good bit of time on the beach with the children, I spoiled it a bit by drinking strong bitter in a Scottish pub and then flaking out, in bed in the afternoon. After we would put the children to bed, Kathleen and I would drink Bacardi and Coke, which could be bought for as little as ten shillings. I got to enjoy Bacardi but I did not drink it when I got home. The apartment was a dump and we were glad to leave it, Kathleen cutting loose with the owner before we left. Kathleen has a furious temper and you should see her when she lets rip. She is the one person that I am really afraid of, maybe that is why I fell for her the first day.

Charles Haughey was elected Taoiseach in December 1979 and this had huge implications for me, work-wise. He had been elected on the promise that he would reduce public expenditure, which was given effect in the budget of 1980. The Department of Finance, in pursuit of this new mandate, rang Deirdre Raul in my section asking, what our contractual building commitments were for 1980. I got a fright not knowing the first thing about budgeting for the building programme and I am afraid I ducked for cover and gave a seriously understated figure. When this figure was published in the 1980 budget, this left us short by about five million and as result, it would not be possible for any projects to go ahead for the entire of that year. This had very serious implications, politically, for the Minister for Education, the otherwise genial John Wilson.

Seamus Mac an tSaoir, my new Principal Officer was put in charge of sorting out the mess and he took to the task with ruthless frankness though, at heart, he was a kind man and was later to become very supportive of me. He was a great Gaelgeoir, a member of the Vincent de Paul society and a staunch supporter of Fianna Fáil. His son Peadar was to die in a freak accident in the French Alps in 1981. Peadar was a civil servant with a promising career ahead of him—he was twenty-four when he died and Seamus never got over it. Seamus is eighty-eight now and though he had a reputation for being strict, he was always fair and believed in a huge work ethic. Seamus had a huge influence on me and was to advise me about my drinking after I had a near-seizure from overindulgence in Kerry in 1981. When I meet him now, I tell him how long I am off it and thank him for his words of caution.

The first few weeks of 1980 were spent going though the budgetary figures and trying to establish exactly how bad the position was. It was my first lapse as an Assistant Principal, indeed, I could never manage budgets properly despite Seamus' experienced instruction. Even in later years, I always overran the allocation, which ironically was welcomed by politicians, though not the Minister. This got me into frequent trouble with the top brass in the Department of Education when I moved there with the Schools' Building Programme in 1985. Even in years of great financial stringency, I always managed to overrun.

Kathleen, the children and myself went to Yugoslavia for our summer holidays in 1980. We were staying in a campus in Dubrovnik and it was idyllic with a pre-first world war ambience in the local villages. We got a bad fright when Fionnuala got pneumonia and we had to rush her to a hospital in the town where the facilities were obsolete. With the help of injections and tablets, we got her back to full health. I did not drink much on that holiday and swam every day. I was not too impressed with the regime in force in the campus, it was so military. You could not even tip the waiters or fraternise with them. 1980 was well before the civil-war which was to destroy the country and lead to appalling genocide and ethnic cleansing. We all enjoyed ourselves but the flight was rocky on the way home, Kathleen vowing never to fly again, and the children asleep for the whole journey.

On my return it was the 1981 estimates time and under Seamus' guidance, with his project-by-project projections, I did not make bags of it this time. As a result, we got a huge allocation for 1981, too much, in fact, and we had to hand money back by the end of the year, which was more frowned on by the Minister than overspending.

In April 1980, I reeled off ten poems, which to me were not any good. I take a critical view of anything I do and the poems fell short of my aspirations. Well, the poems were rejected by the Irish Times in the event.

I love April with the whole summer to look forward to and I was in great form when I wrote these poems, somewhat elated indeed, though I was still taking my tablets. I was on Melleril by then, which has the same impact as Largaclyl but had not the same adverse side effects. I was to on this drug up to the nineties when the authorities took it off the market because there was a risk of heart failure from it. "Now they tell me," I said to my doctor.

There were two tragic deaths in the office that year which caused a pall of gloom. Seamus' son died and Jim Sammon's son was killed in a road accident, aged seventeen, on his way to work to a job which Jim got for him. Jim was a Clerk of Works in Schools' Division and was a mad Dublin fan, madder than I was. He gesticulated wildly when making a point and had a stutter. He was highly respected in his job and kept schools' builders on their toes. He never let them away with shoddy work and the builders were wary of him. He made a lot on travelling expenses and must have missed that when he retired. I had the honour of making his going-away presentation with Mary O'Rourke, the Minister for Education, being present. Jim is in hospital now with a stroke but I can still see him in full-flight making a point about work, about politics or football. He was a great worker and began his career as a carpenter when he was fourteen.

PART FIVE
1981–1990

AVING GOT THE BUDGET RIGHT FOR 1981, the work was easy, free of political pressure though the load was heavy, the staff having to work like beavers. Relations with the architects began to turn round and I would insist that administrative staff would have a say in a project without impinging on the architects' rights. In all my years in Schools' Division, I ensured that architects, engineers, inspectors and administration would have an input into the work. It took a while to turn the old practice of architects having the only say around—and I regard it as an achievement on my part.

I was supposed to go to West Kerry for a week in July (on my own) but I had to put this off because of Seamus' bereavement. I eventually went in the last week in July and it was an unmitigated disaster. I was booked into Granville's Hotel in Ballyferriter for the week and I travelled by train to Killarney on the Saturday with the intention of going to the Munster final between Cork and Kerry the following day. I drank my fill on the Saturday and was curing myself in my hotel early the following morning. I met two of Kathleen's brothers, Michael and Martin, before the match when I was well tanked up and then had a further skinful. So when I got up the following morning with the intention of getting a train to Tralee at eleven o'clock, I first called into the Tatler Jack's pub for a cure. I then met a crowd of lads who had heard me singing in Dublin and they asked me to sing, something I could not resist. I stayed in that pub the whole day barely making the last train to Tralee. I caused great amusement on the bus to Ballyferriter by singing the whole way. I drank morning, noon and night for the whole week and I met two middle-aged women who wanted to take care of me. So I let them, entirely innocent, I can assure you. They insisted that I eat and looked after me all day. When I got back to work on the Monday I was in an awful state; I was running up the steps from the canteen when I got a near-seizure, which alarmed Seamus Mac an tSaoir. As I said previously, he told me to watch my drinking and that it would kill me—truly a good friend and mentor. Seamus was not much of a drinker but enjoyed a drop of whiskey.

There was one item, which caused me trouble in 1981/82 through no fault of my own. In July 1981, the Department of Education who controlled the Schools' building purse-strings introduced a scheme, which would enable schools' managers to execute works on their own initiative, without seeking the advice of the OPW. This incensed the OPW architects and engineers and one engineer, Tom Kiernan, was particularly scornful. The Department of Education gave Schools' Managers the option of doing work under the new scheme or going through the OPW in the normal way. So when our office was asked to advise managers, though otherwise the works fell within the remit of the new scheme, I would ask an architect or engineer for advice and recommendations. So I continued to send such engineering cases to Tom Kiernan who refused to handle them saying that they came within the terms of the new scheme. I sent him many such cases believing that it fell to us to deal with them as if the terms of the new scheme did not apply. I thought I had made it clear to Tom that we should continue to give advice when asked to do so. I did this on individual files and orally on many occasions. But Tom would not budge and the files began to pile up. Tom was saying I had not put the matter in writing but I thought I had done enough. This impasse went on well into 1982 and, in a fit of pique one day, Tom sent all the files, which had been in piles in his room to Seamus, with a note one each one of them—"Oral Instructions." This made the normally gentle Seamus very angry and I was getting upset too, as I felt my reputation was being tarnished by the situation. Seamus directed me to bring all the files back to Tom's office but I refused banging a file on the table. Seamus was now in a fury but I turned on my heels and left his room. Tom kept up his vendetta for years and even after Seamus retired in 1982, Tom would tackle him after Mass shouting "Oral Instructions." Tom could not stand the administration and once said to me in the height of the ongoing row, "We were lice on the backs of the professionals." Tom also had a "thing" against consulting engineers and waged a campaign against them for years even writing to the Department of Finance and the Comptroller and Auditor General about their shortcomings as he saw them. This was indeed incongruous on Tom's part because it was he who had recommended the appointment of these consultants in the first place. Generally, relations between professional and administrative sides were always a bit strained, though each side knew they needed each other.

Apart from the Tom Kiernan situation, I got on well with my professional colleagues as long as they recognised that administration had a crucial role to play in Schools' work and they gradually came around to acknowledging our position. I would not let any of my staff to be treated as dogsbodies. I had no problem in asserting myself when it came to the crunch. While I would be naturally diffident, I always defended my staff when I though it warranted and I think I was respected by the professionals because of that.

I was now Branch Secretary of the Association of Higher Civil Servants but the issues did not seem to be as important anymore. It always seemed to be about pay and promotion with no major principle involved. But there was one major Union matter in September 1982 involving principles, which engulfed the Office for a few weeks. I will deal with it now. Paddy Condon was Chairman of the Branch. I was Secretary and John Mahony who was later to become Chairman of the OPW itself was its leading light. John was very ambitious and made no bones of the fact.

Round about September the then chairman of the OPW retired and Paschal Scanlon got the job. However, contrary to normal custom and practice, the consequent vacancy at Commissioner level was filled from the outside; a man called Brendan Scully of the Department of Finance was imposed on the OPW from that Department. The Unions' response was swift and emphatic; the new incumbent would be blacked and a campaign of non-co-operation was prepared which involved a work-to-rule, John Mahony being the main Architect. Our Branch Committee got the co-operation of the other administrative unions and soon normal working was at a standstill; everything had to be in writing and this proved to be very effective. No compromise seemed possible. The union demanded that Mr. Scully, an ordinary decent man, be sent back to the Department of Finance and his appointment rescinded. We insisted that he would be replaced in-house. The Department of Finance, naturally, could not concede these demands and impasse ensued for about six weeks. The work-to-rule ensured that Mr. Scully did not even get paid, ruthless indeed, but we were determined to stand firm. The Department of Finance agreed to meet a deputation from the Union and John Mahony and Paddy Condon were selected to represent the Branch. I was, somewhat, disappointed that I was not asked to go but I know, deep down, that John Mahony would be more able to argue our case. I heard after that it was a fiery meeting with Mahony at one point saying that the Department of Finance was treating our staff "like coolies in India."

Then a breakthrough came in November 1982 when the short-lived Fianna Fáil Government was on the eve of leaving office. Sylvester Barrett, the Minister, met a union delegation saying he did not want to leave office with the dispute unresolved. With that result an agreement was hammered out which, though a compromise, was acceptable to our union. It was agreed that Mr. Scully would stay in his post but there would be an immediate appointment at that level in-house; with the consequent filling of the Principal vacancy plus two new Principal posts and filling of all consequent vacancies. Cyril Griffith, my old boss from Personnel, got the Assistant General Secretary promotion and Fergus got one of the Principal posts. Though the executive officers union called it a sell-out, our union thought it was an honourable settlement.

Fergus and the rest of the lads were pleased with their promotions and Cyril Griffith was to become my boss yet again and I immediately set out to impress him remembering the days in Personnel when I did not shine. I was now on top of my job, the budget was ample and I had learned a lot from Seamus who retired in the middle of 1982 to be replaced by the irrepressible Paddy Condon, who was not as strict as Seamus was. I needed someone to be firm with me but I was too friendly with Paddy to achieve this. In 1982, with the Tom Kiernan saga in full spate, I went for a month's holiday to America.

For the six months before I went on holiday, I had been getting very fit. At the beginning of 1982, I decided that I was going to run in the marathon in October. I had been training in the health-studio on a regular basis but now I started to jog a few nights a week starting with a short distance and then increasing my mileage. By July I was jogging over twenty miles in a session a few times a week and I was very fit, down to 140 pounds weight and I was pleased. I was convinced that if I kept up my progress that I would run the marathon in about four hours. I left for America at the end of July with Kathleen on that assumption, leaving the children with her parents in Cork.

I have had bad memories of the trip still, though it is nearly a quarter of a century since I made it. First of all a month was too long and I got homesick. We were met at the airport by Dick, Aunt Mollie's grandson and it was a round of welcoming parties. All my aunts where alive then and their hospitality could not have been warmer. We stayed with Auntie Mollie and her husband Tal for the first few nights. Then at the weekend we went to stay with my cousin Sue and her husband, Paul, at their holiday home by the sea which was like the Bahamas. But I drank too much the first night, consuming nearly thirty cans of beer. I felt then and still feel it, that Paul was disgusted. We went to Long Beach Island the following morning and I could not wait to sneak away in my running gear to get a drink. I had put twenty dollars in my runner for the purpose and spent the day on my own drinking steadily. When I got back to the beach, they were all gone and I promptly fell asleep and woke up late in the evening. The silence the following morning was palpable as we headed off to Auntie Kitty's where there was a party thrown in our honour.

We visited Anita, Sue's sister in Hartford and she was very hospitable. Her husband had been injured in the Korean War. He drove me down to an Irish Club and I sang and drank all day. I was very drunk when I got home. I do not want to turn this memoir into a drunkalogue but drinking was a large part of that holiday and a large part of my life generally. We got the train down to Washington DC from Trenton and we stayed in a posh hotel. We went to Arlington, which really impressed me, visited the Senate, and the Smithsonian museum as well as the National Archives. I made a disgrace of myself in the Dubliner bar in the city and Kathleen would not speak to me the following morning.

So the memories are not good of that visit. I knew all my relatives could not wait for my father to come—he was arriving at Kennedy the day I was leaving and I met him at the airport with Gerry—it was very emotional indeed. I think my aunts were indulgent of me on my visit, as if I was John the Baptist being the precursor to Jesus. Maybe this is an exaggeration. I felt so badly about the trip; even though I am not drinking now, I do not think I will ever go to the States again. I did a lot—went to Broadway, went up the Empire State Building, visited the Lincoln centre and the Kennedy centre in Washington, mastered the subway but I cannot help feeling now that, somehow, it was a missed opportunity. My father had a ball there with parties every night for him—he was to die the following year. I came home from America two stone overweight which meant I was not fit enough to run in the marathon and in the event I never did make it to the starting line, let alone finish it. But, on my return, I went to the club and remained an active member until it closed in 1985. My present weight is a respectable 160 pounds but I do not train any more.

Daddy was in the last year of his life when he came back from America in September 1982. The prostate cancer was spreading and he was invariably in awful pain. We sold the house in Cabra Road that year and my father had moved in with Mollie to spend his last days in her house. He had been lonely and desolate on his own in Cabra Road and was unable to properly look after himself. He was still mourning my mother and was a broken man. When I was doing the paperwork on the selling of the house, I came across the deeds of the property he so proudly bought in 1952. Though there were some happy days there, there was too much sorrow for me to have good memories of it. I am not bitter but the memories are anything but sweet. Or maybe the fault is down to my warped retrospection.

In July 1983, we found the perfect place in West Kerry to spend our holidays in the future, Ventry with it s beautiful beach and Paud Quinn's bar, the Clasach, with Mount Eagle towering over it all. In fact we have gone there as a family every year since 1983 mainly because of the beach and the walks but particularly because of the generous hospitality of Paud Quinn, the owner of the Ventry Inn. When I picked the area, I told Danny Lynch, a native of Dingle, and who is now PRO for the GAA, I wanted a soft sandy beach with a pub overlooking it, so he selected Ventry for me. It is the nearest thing to Nirvana, this side of the great divide. I wrote a song called *Quinn's of Ventry* the following year, which is still popular. Kathleen always asks me to sing it when she is a bit tipsy at a party. The bar is kept immaculately clean by Paud's wife, Sheila, and they have two sons and a daughter. I drank the first week in Quinn's in 1983 and have not had a drink there since. We rent a house each year and often planned to buy or build one but never did. If I were to opt for cremation when I die, I would wish my ashes to be scattered on Ventry Harbour. It is Kathleen's favourite spot of all the places she has been and she has been all over the world in recent years.

In 1984, Páidi Ó Sé, the famous footballer, opened a pub in the nearby Árd an Bóthair and we go there too but not as often as Quinn's. The high point of any holiday for Kathleen is eating out—she is a bit of an expert on food and relishes a gourmet meal, while little pleases me. Our children were young in 1983 and came to Ventry with us until they suddenly stopped and now they are coming as adults with their friends who stay in a big rented home with us in Caherbullig, owned by Mr. & Mrs. Jack Griffin, a lovely couple. We meet Sean Conlon, a nephew of Mr. Conlon's, the geography teacher in O'Connells long ago. Sean taught in O'Connells too and he recently retired after nearly forty years service. Noreen and Joe often holidayed in West Kerry but Gerry never did. He prefers Portugal, where he has a time-share apartment.

But Ventry with its walk over the Clasagh to be greeted by the Great Blasket rising majestically from the sea, or the long journey around Slea head and Clochar on the road to Ballyferriter with its raging surf, all hold a special place in my heart. In the eighties, we would have a drink in Kane's bar in Ballyferriter and old Donal would help us with our faltering Irish and then at closing time we would head for Granville's Hotel where the dawn would greet the midnight with sounds of songs and politics. Bertie Ahern and John A. Murphy would often give a bar or two, John not knowing when to stop. You could go to

Kruger's where Padraig O Neill is still in charge and you would walk back over the Clasagh to Ventry village, permanent in its timelessness, surely paradise. Though I have now made Riva Del Garda in Italy my second holiday-home where Fionnuala has been working and living for the past five years, Ventry is still number one for me and Kathleen despite the vagaries of our Irish summers.

Dublin won the All-Ireland in 1983 when they beat Galway in a battle royal with twelve men. I wrote a song about it, which was published in the Dublin GAA magazine but drank like a lunatic for the week having won a big bet at fifteen-to-one from Danny Lynch. I have not had a drink on All-Ireland day since then.

My father was dying then and in great agony as we frequently ferried him to Hospital. He would be in such pain he would try to get out of the car. He was moved to Blanchardstown Hospital where he died on 27th November 1983, the week Gerry's club— Scoil Uí Chonaill—won the county championship with Gerry as manager. As my father lay in death's throes, all the family was around him including Conor and Fionnuala. Conor was very moved at the significance of it all. Bill was there too when my father died at nine o'clock. He was brought to Blanchardstown Church for the funeral service and is buried in Glasnevin with my mother in repose together for eternity.

I drank a fair bit after the funeral but with great dignity being hugely conscious of the solemnity of the occasion. Though we had had our differences, I mourned him as any son would. He was a great and gifted man—his problem was he could not communicate with his children until he got older and when we were settled. I went over to O'Dwyers in the evening with Joe Fahey and Matt O'Dwyer offered me money but I refused it, thinking, however, that it was a decent gesture. My only regret about the funeral was that we did not get somebody to play a lament over his grave but this was really a celebration of a great and good life, an exultation of something achieved.

When I returned to the office myself, Paddy Condon and Cyril Griffith were summoned up to the Minister's room, Joe Bermingham who was complaining bitterly that we were not looking after his constituency properly. We all sat down in the Boardroom where Joe delivered his tirade, pointing the finger at me. When Cyril saw me getting agitated, he gently put his hand on my knee in an effort to ensure I kept calm under Joe's ferocious onslaught. Joe did not know that my father was only dead a few days, otherwise he would have been gentler with me. We all left the room shaken. Joe Bermingham was the Labour deputy for Kildare but, like all politicians, he nurtured his patch. He was a gruff countryman but was completely incorruptible. When he fell out with the Labour party on a point of principle and resigned his position as Minister, Charlie Haughey tried to bribe him for his vote offering him a well-paid sinecure in a semi-State body. Joe, typical of this principled man, refused. I met Joe in Croke Park a few days after the meeting and we had a good laugh. Joe would not bear a grudge and neither would I.

In all my years working with politicians—and more of that later—I was never asked to do anything remotely corrupt though I was dealing with building projects with their reputation for corruption, tenders for building projects for example. Joe and I were to become close friends when he was a backbencher and I never mentioned my father's death to him.

I was on top of the work then, though at Estimates time I wrote to the Department of Education projecting an overrun for 1983 of three million on the allocation but I did not care. As Charlie Haughey famously said, "A million is a figure you'd easily lose in a tot," and he should know.

1984 was the year of the Orwellian nightmare—I was an almost obsessive reader of Orwell and have read all his works and everything that has been written about him. After a bad binge on 31 of December 1983, I took the pledge and vowed to stay off the drink for the whole of 1984. I was to last one hundred days, an all-time record for me at that point but I went back on it with a bang after Easter. I know now through psychological counselling and a programme of recovery, left to your own wiles and devices, it is impossible to stay stopped. So I tried to abstain again and again only to break out with greater ferocity, the dry periods getting shorter and shorter. On 1 July 1984, I finally surrendered and acknowledged that I was powerless over alcohol if I was relying on willpower alone. On that momentous day I sought and got help. For the first time in my life, I admitted my powerlessness and went into a twelve-step programme of recovery, which has, in the main, kept me alcohol-free until the present day. I would like to tell you that I have been completely dry since July 1984, but I am afraid I have had the odd slip over the years, as alcohol is a cunning and subtle foe. I was baffled by the obsessional nature of the condition and, in early 1985, I went to St. Dympna's beside the Gorman, an alcohol treatment-centre where Dr. Stephenson was my adviser. He had a huge reputation in the field and I listened and learned. He put me on Anti-Buze, a tablet that if you drank on it, you would have all the symptoms of a heart attack. He strongly and laconically said "I wouldn't try it if I were you" but I knew I would not stay sober on Anti-Buze alone, so I took to the Recovery Programme with great gusto and, in the main, it has kept me free of drink for twenty-two years now. I now have a Higher Power in my life that I choose to call God and I have done the twelve-step programme to the best of my ability with the guidance of a counsellor. I have admitted my wrongs to a priest and they were many and have made my amends to Kathleen in particular for all the hurt I have caused. The programme teaches you how to stay off drink "one day at a time" and I know now that it is the first drink that does the damage. Lift the phone, they say, before you lift a drink. I try to do that but as I have said, alcohol is indeed a fatal attraction for me still. Indeed, the obsession has never left me.

I would like to be able to say that this was the end of my problems but it was not and there were to be a number of serious challenges for me in the future, particularly from a work

point-of-view, which was to badly affect my mental health. You
see drink was not my only problem, though it did me serious
damage over the years. I still had a deep rooted sense of insecurity and obsessional compulsive behaviour which later nearly
brought me back to the fringes of insanity. But now I did not
have the crutch of alcohol, dubious as it was, to sustain me in
the late eighties and nineties. I had never got over my deeply felt
low self-esteem and conviction that I had no ability. But there
were external forces at work too, which almost brought about
my downfall.

In early 1984, the Government, led by Garret Fitzgerald,
took a decision, which was to have far-reaching implications for
my career. With Gemma Hussey as Minister for Education, the
Cabinet took a decision to transfer the whole school building
programme to the Department of Education. The Commissioners of Public Works did not take kindly to this decision and for
the most of 1984 fought a campaign to keep Schools' Division in
the OPW. I was a crucial part of the team lead by Cyril Griffith,
spearheading the campaign even suggesting a transition period
of seven years for the transfer.

Naturally, the Government did not accept this and in early
1985, the Taoiseach, losing his patience, decided that the whole
Schools' Buildings programme be transferred to the Department
as early as possible in 1985. It was left to the two Departments to
make the arrangements for transfer. The Department did not in
fact want the Schools' Programme lock, stock and barrel but had
no option but to comply with the Government's directive. They
said it was a condition of their acceptance of the transfer, that I
would transfer with the work as I had the necessary experience
to oversee the whole project and I had a good reputation with the
top brass in the Department. I had mixed feelings about leaving;
I had enjoyed the family atmosphere in the OPW, which gave me
the security I needed. But I enjoyed the schools' work and feared
if I did not go that I might be put in a section I felt I was not able
for. I still had those fears of inadequacy. I was also concerned

about promotion prospects in the new Department and I went to see Donie Garvey, who worked in Personnel there—he is a brother-in-law of Tony Forde and I had often met him socially. He brought me through the staff list and I figured that I would have as good a chance of promotion in the Department to Principal Officer as I would in the OPW. This enabled me to reach a decision so I agreed to transfer with effect from July 1985 with the rest of my staff to move at the end of the year.

There was a huge air of expectancy and nervousness when I arrived in the Buildings' Branch with the Department's staff very apprehensive. Paddy Heneghan was my Principal Officer and he gave me a great welcome. We were to get on well for a few years but this honeymoon period did not last beyond 1987 through circumstances for which neither of us was responsible. Paddy was a great teacher and a hard worker but was far too cautious. He once said to me that he had an escape clause in every sentence, which was not much good to a school manager who just wanted to know when his school was going ahead. The Department staff needed a lot of assurance but cooperated as well as they could.

Enda Kenny was the Minister of State at the time and I was to get to know him very well. I often felt he never took himself seriously enough except when it came to minding his own patch in Mayo.

The biggest difference in the Department of Education was the daily involvement with politicians. Three days a week were taken up with Parliamentary Questions and Adjournment Debates. Under Paddy's guidance, I soon became a dab-hand at answering them. Paddy would say, when hammering out a reply to an Adjournment Debate, "Let's throw more sand in their eyes," meaning every bit of it, which appalled me. As somebody who had ambitions to be a creative writer, I valued crystal-clear prose. At first, I liked working with Paddy—he was definitely a safe pair of hands and often referred to the Department as if indeed it was not responsible for what was done in its name.

In April 1985, I had my first real go at creative writing for which I always had an ambition. I wrote a short-story in Cork called *Long Night's Journey in to Day* and I entered it in a competition. Having done a large number of writing workshops, I now know that it was not well written so I did not win the competition but I was slightly disappointed. They did not discourage me from writing and I wrote a good few more, which were well received in workshops, though I never tried to get them published. The idea of failure seems to act for me as a disincentive to actually trying to get published. But I continued to write short-stories often not bothering to get them typed at all. Perhaps I had a death wish in my writing efforts but I kept it up until I discovered that my strength was in my dialogue. So I eventually started writing plays, mostly monologues, which lead to my first real success. I wrote a one-act play in 1991 called *Christmas at Home* and it was performed at Listowel Writer's Week in 1993, having won a prize in a competition in a writing festival in Co. Kilkenny. This was to be my first and, to date, only success at writing. I continued to persevere at short stories and, in 1992, I wrote ten in the space of three months but never even bothered to get them typed. I am writing monologues in the form of one-act plays since. They say that the fact that you want to write does not necessarily mean you are a writer let alone a successful one, which I wanted dearly to be. But at least I was trying. I tried to assure myself if I could only bother to take the necessary quantum-leap to go and seek publication of my stories or performance of my plays, I would succeed. My efforts have always been received well in literary workshops but then inaction followed.

Work was going well and in January 1986, my staff and the professional cadre of schools were amalgamated into the Department's new Building Unit. I still had most of my old staff and we all now acted as if the change had not taken place at all. Whatever happened, the work had to go on. This came first. 1986 was to be a good year for me from the point of view of work and life generally. I was still sober and keeping to my recovery programme and Kathleen and my children were all well. In short, life was good. I worked a lot of unpaid overtime in that period, including Saturdays and Sundays.

In 1986 Gerry and I, as executors of my father's will, sold his land in Leitrim with farcical consequences. The family had asked Gerry if he wanted the property and when he said no, we decided that we had no option but to put it on the market. We engaged a solicitor and a local auctioneer for the sale. When the bidding started, to Gerry's and my dismay, Rosemarie started to bid. This caused us great embarrassment as we felt that our Solicitor thought that Rosemarie was a plant to put up the selling price. However, a neighbouring farmer bought the property, outbidding Rosemarie at the last minute. Gerry and I were greatly relieved until Rosemarie spent the whole day trying to buy the property back from the successful bidder. It was a real farce but Rosemarie eventually succeeded in buying some of the land and the house for the same price that the successful bidder had paid for the whole lot. The net effect was that he had secured the land he wanted for nothing. Years afterwards and only recently there was to be a good outcome for this debacle. Conor, my son, has now bought the holding of a house on five acres from Rosemarie, thereby, ensuring that the premises will stay in the Rowley family for future generations. The Rowleys have been there for nearly three hundred years and Conor's action has ensured that the family will be there for at least a while longer. My father and Uncle Paddy would be pleased, as indeed is Bill who is now eighty, still going strong. Conor is going to modernise the old homestead and use it as a holiday home to his wife Ashley's delight. Truly a satisfactory outcome, though it took years, to an otherwise disastrous situation. I hope Conor's descendants will see the importance of keeping the house in the family in the future.

In his will, my father left fifty thousand pounds in cash to be divided equally amongst the seven of us. I first invested my share of seven thousand pounds in the Investment Bank of Ireland but, under pressure from the bank where I had an equivalent overdraft, I cleared the debt unknown to Kathleen. She was still under the illusion that my inheritance was earning interest in the Investment Bank. Though I was not drinking now I was still inclined to be profligate when it came to money and soon ran up another overdraft, much to the annoyance of my bank manager. Around Christmas time in 1986, I lodged my usual pay-cheque and went to collect a chequebook to tide us over the Christmas but, much to my dismay, the bank refused to give me one. It was Christmas and I needed money but the bank said I had run out of credit and they out of patience. It was hard to blame them. In despair, I called to Gerry and broke down like a recalcitrant schoolboy. He gave me an awful dressing-down and a lecture about the need to mend my ways. Before leaving, however, he gave me two hundred pounds, which while substantial, was still not enough to get us over the Christmas.

I reluctantly went back to the bank and almost got down on my knees in supplication asking a young girl for two hundred, which she eventually gave me. I was near to tears, indeed pathetic. You see I had a thing about money and being a good provider (which I was) especially at Christmas. When giving the bulk of the money to Kathleen, I said there was a strike at the printing-press in the bank, hence no chequebook. I was in total despair over Christmas—how would I tell Kathleen especially about the £7,000, which she still thought was safely invested not to mention the overdraft of the same amount. I kept up a brave front until the end of January 1987 and made up my mind that the only way to face Kathleen was to get drunk. I headed out the side-door of the Office with this intention but was met by a fellow who was also on the dry and I told him what I was going to do. He persuaded me to go for a coffee and as I held the cup in my hand, I got a moment of clarity about the futility of drinking as a solution. So, I returned to the office and rang home and Fionnuala answered. "Get your mother," I said. I was now crying. I told Kathleen "I'm in trouble, come in for me."

When we sat in the car and I poured my troubles out to her and extent of my indebtedness, all she said was "Is that all?" to my great relief. What a woman—she was minus fourteen thousand pounds and that is all she said. Kathleen is a great manager, deplores debt, and is now in charge of our finances. I got a substantial lump sum when I retired in 2004 and it is safely invested in our joint names. I will always be a bad manager of money but in Kathleen's hands, our money is safe.

In 1986, we were heading for an allocation overrun of about five million but, by December, I knew that I had underestimated it by a further million. Paddy Heneghan was working on a submission to the Department of Finance seeking approval to this overrun and, one morning in Bewleys, I was shaking with fear about the further overrun. Despite my fear, I decided to tell him, otherwise, we would run out of money before Christmas when pressure for payments was greatest. Paddy was at his typewriter working on his finance submission with me standing over him. I was nearly shaking as Paddy said, "Read over that," handing me his script. I got to the last paragraph and said, almost casually, that the figure of five million should read six. Without another word, Paddy took out his Tippex and changed five to six. What a man. He was a great boss and it was a pity that things were to go sour between us in 1987/88.

In 1986, I had two incidents with Enda Kenny, then Minister of State in charge of School Buildings, which still stand out. One day he asked me to go over to see Dick Spring who was Minister for Energy and who wanted an update on schools' projects in Kerry. I knew that these cases were about to go ahead shortly but Enda told me "Tell him nothing." "But Minister, I can't. These projects are about to proceed," I said. "Stall him," was Enda's reply. I went to see Dick Spring and bluffed him for an hour—he was bewildered, poor man. When I reported back to Enda he said, "Draft me a letter for the local Fine Gael Deputies telling them that the cases are going ahead." "But what about Dick Spring?" I said. "We'll tell him later," Enda said.

Another day in 1986, Enda was receiving a deputation from a north County Dublin School who were campaigning for a new school and looking for the go-ahead. Enda was usually good with deputations, almost charming, but on this occasion, his charm failed him. He said something to a lady member of the deputation, which to her was patronising, even offensive. In a fit of anger, she threw her file on the table. Enda was perplexed and when the deputation left, he asked me "What was the matter with her?" I could not tell that he had been patronising as you had to be on your guard with Ministers, so I just said "She was just upset at the lack of progress on the school." After the project proceeded, I met the woman on the train—she was very embarrassed by the incident. I smiled and said, "Just write to the Minister and thank him".

The Fine Gael led coalition departed from office at the end of January 1987. Before they did, they left a big problem for the Department. On the day before they left, Enda Kenny directed that all projects planned and budgeted for in 1987 were to be released to tender and contract. Paddy Heneghan was on sick-leave at that time, so I went to Brendan Meehan, the Assistant Secretary General looking for advice. Brendan was an easygoing type and it was hard to ruffle him. He was, as usual, reading the Irish Times and smoking when I called to see him. All he said was "Make sure you cover yourself." This was not much help I thought as I returned to my room. I then rang Paddy at home and he hammered out a letter to be sent to the schools with the good news—the wily Paddy ensuring that there were enough safety clauses in the letter. These letters were issued to all concerned on the day the Government left office. It appeared that the money for 1987 was committed before the new Fianna Fáil Government took office in February and it was our job to break the bad news to the new Minister, the formidable Mary O'Rourke. The new Government took office with great expectation on the public's part. It was led by Charlie Haughey who felt mandated to get the public finances back in order and the only way to do this was by cutbacks, which the Civil Service felt honour-bound to resist. The Minister, Mary O'Rourke, and the Minister of State, Frank Fahey, soon asked to see us, which Paddy and I were not looking forward to. In advance of the meeting, Paddy prepared a project by project list of all the cases released by the previous administration. It showed that all the allocation for 1987 was fully committed.

Needless to say, neither Minister was pleased with Mary O'Rourke being particularly incensed. To tell a new Government that they had no room for manoeuvre in their first year in office was a hard thing to do. But Paddy, in particular, stuck to his guns in his lecturing tones. I spoke when asked to do so by the Minister and I must have impressed her as she asked to see me, through Dave Gordon, her able private secretary, a few days afterwards. I did not tell Paddy when I went in trepidation to see the Minister. She was always gracious and courteous to me, anyway, but she was a no-nonsense and formidable woman and I had great respect for her. At her request, I went through the list of projects, which had been committed to tender and contract and I told her that at our peril, we could not go back on them. As it happened none of the cases were actually ready for release at that point as the formalities had not yet been completed. So I suggested to the Minister that she could write a letter to all concerned at the actual point of release – "Having reviewed the matter etc." she would say in her letter. In that way the Minister could make up lost ground on the previous Government's action and approve the projects and get some credit.

This was the beginning of my relationship with Mary O'Rourke, which was the most rewarding official experience of my entire career. It lasted until she left as Minister for Education in 1991. It was also frustrating and right through 1988 it had to be clandestine vis-a-vis Paddy Heneghan. I was still his junior and he kept a sharp eye on my activities.

Just before the National Teachers' Annual Conference at Easter 1987, Paddy sent the Minister the list of the released cases with a detailed breakdown of expenditure proposed. On the list Paddy had put aside a sum of two million pounds for a new painting grants scheme for National Schools scheduled to be introduced that year, which in the event never got off the ground, which was to give rise to a shortfall in expenditure that year. This was to have serious repercussions for Paddy in particular but they were fortuitous for me.

Imagine my dismay when I bought a copy of the Irish Independent on the Tuesday after Easter. Paddy's list appeared in glorious print on the front page. I knew at once that it was the Minister who released the list as she could confidently tell the INTO, the teachers' union, that all the 1987 budget was committed by the previous administration with the effect that she had no room for manoeuvre that year. This was to embarrass the Minister at year-end when we had to hand back the two million, which was not spent on the painting grants scheme. I tried, vainly, before I went on holidays in August 1987 to show how the unspent money could be spent on other projects. Indeed, I went into the office at 6:00 AM. the morning of my departure to prepare a list of schools with expenditure allocations amounting to two million pounds but Paddy, to my annoyance, did not act on the list. This was to be a fatal mistake on Paddy's part.

In 1987, I took an important step in pursuit of my writing career. I went to Listowel Writers' Week for the first time and have been going there every year since. The Writers' Week has been the most wonderful experience that I ever enjoyed. I enrolled in a short fiction workshop with Azuo Ishiguro in charge and it was nothing short of fantastic, a new and rewarding experience for me. I took part in all the chief events and over the years, I have made life-long friends from all over the world. As an activist, I threw myself into the new adventure with abandon. I think that I have made a contribution too. For a few years I gave one-man shows and, more recently, I have been MC at Poet's Corner. It is not for me to say if I have been successful but I do my best to be involved. The staff of the Office, Eilish and Maura, and the

Committee have always given me a great welcome and backup. Listowel Writers' Week is a huge part of my social life and only death or incapacity would stop me going in the future. I have always gone to a workshop in an effort to improve my writing skills and it was through workshops that I learned where my creative skills lay. But there is no real substitute for actual writing, and I am remiss in this still, never bothering to get my efforts typed or send them for publishing. In fact, I have not written much for the past few years, and this memoir, such as it is, is an effort to get back on track.

We went to Ventry, as usual, for our summer holidays in 1987 and enjoyed it immensely, though work was always at the back of my mind. I had taken the month of August off and ended up at the Fleadh Cheoil in Listowel where I sang my heart out in the Horseshoe Bar. There I met David Carmichael for the first time who was to become a lifelong friend. He married Fionnuala Cassidy whom we met at the Kilkenny Fleadh in 1988, after a long courtship and I was at their wedding in his native Glasgow in 2004.

In Kilkenny also in 1988, we met Tom and Anne Clarke from Co. Derry and we are still friends. I often visit them in their home and they have two grown-up sons. Anne is Fionnuala's best friend and it was I who introduced Fionnuala to David for the first time in Kilkenny.

The rest of my work in 1987 was taken up with Parliamentary Questions and meeting deputations with the Minister which were always lively affairs with schools' authorities vehemently arguing their cases. I often took deputations with Frank Fahey, the junior Minister , who found it hard to hold the line. You always got the impression that his mind was elsewhere when you were talking to him and he always arrived late. Still it was hard not to like him. He was very wary of Mary O'Rourke, not for any bad reasons, but as she was the senior Minister with the authority to allow cases to proceed, he had to get her approval for schools in his constituency. He would ask me to make submissions to the Minister making a strong case for approval, which invariably was given.

In September 1987, there was a deputation to the Minister from a school in Co. Kilkenny with Bishop Forristal leading it. The project had been held up by me for financial reasons and I was very nervous going in. I gave, at the Minister's request, details of the cost of the school based on the quantity surveyor's figures. Then the Minister said "Why does it have to be as high as that?" but I defended my position. Then the Bishop came up with an initiative, which had far-reaching implications for the building programme, and which was to benefit me directly and in fact make my name. The Bishop said, "If the school can do it cheaper, will you grant-aid the project? We would have to provide prefabs if the permanent building wasn't proceeding and with the local contribution, the combined money would go a long way to financing the cheaper project." The Minister responded positively and said she would not be found wanting if a cheaper alternative building could be provided by the school provided that standards were satisfactory. This momentous day was to usher in a new phase for primary school building and, despite the capital cutbacks of those years, the Department was not adversely affected.

Even as I got back to my room, Father McEvoy, the school manager, Ben Foley, of my staff, and Tony Sheppard, a rising young architect, were already working on a new and cheaper alternative to the original project. The era of low-cost effective standards of school buildings had started. It was revolutionary and I was to be a big player in the revolution. Myself, Ben and Tony went to visit the school and Tony was ready with a new modified plan. Declan Brennan, the Secretary General of the Department was dubious—he called the visit "a public relations exercise"—but afterwards when I made my report to him and the Minister, I demonstrated that it was not. Furthermore, I showed that the concept of low cost building could be applied successfully to the whole schools programme. The Minister was wildly enthusiastic. What it meant for her was that in a period of severe cutbacks, the school building programme could survive as if nothing had happened. The architects embraced the new era and applied themselves to their new designs with fervour. For some reason or other, Paddy Heneghan was not around to usher in the new dispensation, but he was to implement the new cost-cutting regime vigorously. At the end of 1987, it became evident that the two million pounds, set aside for painting, would not be spent. The Minister was furious as she had gone public to say that the Fine Gael Government had fully committed the allocation. It was a major embarrassment for her and she held Paddy Heneghan responsible. However, she ensured that the unspent money would be carried over into 1988, thus improving the allocation for that year. With the extra money, it was possible to give the go-ahead for projects which, otherwise, would have not proceeded.

Paddy had prepared his programme for the year and had submitted it to the Minister for her approval. It showed limited scope for progress, which concerned the Minister. In February 1988, Dave Gordon met me in the yard of the Department and said the Minister wanted me to prepare an alternative programme. I demurred at first being aware of Paddy's programme but when the Minister says "Jump," you jump. So I consulted with my staff and the Architects and prepared an expanded list of projects, which could go ahead in 1988 and submitted it to Dave.

When I was dealing with the Minister, I always went through him, mainly as a sounding board. Dave was very capable and I got to rely on him. He was a safe pair of hands and could always gauge the Minister's mood. He knew when to approach her and when not to. The Minister called me to her Office on what was to be a fateful day in February 1988, which was to have serious but beneficial repercussions for me career-wise. She told me that she was adopting the programme I had prepared and furthermore she was putting me in charge of Primary Buildings forthwith. I was pleased but shocked—what would Paddy say? None of the top brass told Paddy the situation even when Declan Brennan confirmed to me personally that I was to be in charge, with Paddy blissfully unaware of the position. Declan Brennan said to me "I'm afraid I can't promote you now but you are to carry out the Minister's wishes in every respect." This I did unknown to Paddy, which set in train an appalling period of subterfuge on my part. I was not at fault and I feel bitter still, years later, that the top brass did not tell Paddy the new reality. It was the worst period of my life officially that I had undergone up to that point as being disloyal to my boss was never part of my makeup. I was soon under great strain, living a double-life, hiding cases from Paddy about which I had got directions from the Minister. Paddy soon got suspicious and stopped trusting me and was even reduced to searching my room for files.

One day as I was on the point of breaking and weeping, I told Paddy I wanted a transfer, which seemed to me the only way out. He asked why and I broke down saying the situation was intolerable. But I did not tell him the truth—that was for Brendan Meehan or Declan Brennan to do; it was not my duty to tell Paddy who had given loyal service for nearly forty years that his junior was replacing him. However, the Minister refused to sanction the transfer, saying she wanted me to stay where I was. The impasse lasted for the rest of the year with Paddy becoming undone by his own hand. He sent a circular to all his staff not to act on the Minister's instructions on projects as that would involve breaching a Department of Finance embargo on primary schools projects. This embargo was a response to our chronic overspending which both the Minister and I chose to ignore. I felt strongly that it was our duty to spend our allocation and if new projects did not proceed, we would be handing back a large sum of money at year's end, much more than in 1987. But Paddy was to be the author of his own downfall by sending a copy of his staff-circular to the Minister herself. The Minister's reaction was as swift as it was ruthless—she told Declan Brennan that Paddy was to be removed from primary buildings at once and that the circular be withdrawn. It never was withdrawn by Paddy, a truly remarkable man, too obstinate and inflexible for his own good. He had been a very capable officer and I admired him. Paddy was transferred to Special Education and soldiered on in the Department until he reached sixty-five, the mandatory age for retirement. Though we fell out through no fault of either of us, I had a sneaking regard for him.

In the beginning of 1989, Kevin O'Donnell, the Principal Officer in Post Primary Buildings, a decent and easy-going man, was nominally put in charge of my area but he did not interfere with my operation and let me have my head. Though I was busy, working often sixteen hours a day and at weekends, I was happy, as I was effectively my own boss though, I had not yet been promoted to Principal Officer. We continued working on low-cost buildings and the architects soon developed new prototypes. So it was all systems go, though the budget was severely limited. I got into trouble with the top brass about a huge project, which I had approved, at a cost of one million pounds but I defended my decision with the help of a solicitor as I felt that I had been defamed by Paddy who had been asked by Brendan Meehan for his views. In a vitriolic attack, Paddy did his utmost to damage my reputation but I stood firm in my own defence and I survived.

I relished working on my own and it was the most exhilarating period of my whole career. I was now meeting delegations on my own and I always held out the hope to them that progress was possible, if they would only be patient. I now had a free hand and the only person I had to refer to was the Minister. Though I respected her, I was always on my guard in case I would incur her wrath. Like all politicians, she hated adverse publicity and we had a few disagreements in this regard. "We must stick together, George," she said to me one day after a case got a bad press but which I defended fully. "Yes, Minister" was my reply.

I thought I was doing well and was due for promotion to Principal Officer that year with a vacancy coming up soon. But

I learned on the grapevine that somebody junior to me was to be promoted before me. I was furious, feeling a huge sense of injustice, so I rang Dave Gordon as it was for the Minister to approve promotions and told him the position. Dave spoke to the Minister and while I did not get that promotion—the Minister saying she wanted me to stay in Primary Buildings; soon after, Declan Brennan told me at a social function that he would have good news for me soon. So I was promoted to Principal Officer in June 1989 at the age of forty-five and was to remain in Primary Buildings.

Though I felt I was due the promotion, I knew I owed it all to Mary O'Rourke without whose support, I would not have got it. I often felt, and still do, that I was not popular with the top brass in the Department, believing that they held me responsible for what happened to Paddy Heneghan. But I am still convinced that it was not my fault that I was put in that unenviable position by the top brass who wished to conform to the Minister's wishes—something they had an obligation to do.

There was a general election in May 1989, when Charlie Haughey went to the country in a fit of pique. He formed a Government with the help of the Progressive Democrats. I heard the news on the radio that Mary O'Rourke was being retained as Minister for Education and I was relieved, as I believed that she was the only friend I had at the top level. Events afterwards were to prove me right. Though I have never belonged to a political party and never supported Fianna Fáil, I recognised that I had a staunch ally in Mary O'Rourke and told her so. I have never actually canvassed my own position but I would take no prisoners in securing my own rights. I owe that to my wife and children and my wider family.

I went to Listowel Writers' Week in June 1989 and on holidays to Ventry in August. I was still off the drink and enjoying life; my children were doing well at school and I had no complaints. I was still writing short stories again with later inaction on my part. It was more of the same in 1990 and Mary O'Rourke was still Minister for Education when her brother Brian Lenihan was sacked by the Taoiseach, Charlie Haughey. She was very upset so I did something uncharacteristic for me; I wrote her a letter of sympathy, for which she later thanked me. I have no regrets for pinning my colours to the mast like that. In September 1990, I went to the official opening of Listowel Convent, a magnificent building but of the Rolls Royce type, as the Minister called it at the opening ceremony, which was the last of its kind. We had all by now fully embraced the low-cost concept. We had a ball at the party afterwards and even Paddy Heneghan's presence did not curtail my enjoyment of the day. It was dawn when I got back to Mary Costello, my landlady for over twenty years now. When I go to Listowel, I always stay with Mary and her husband Donie who would look after me as a parent would a child. We have become great friends over the years and I would never contemplate staying anywhere else. They had a major tragedy a few years ago when their only daughter, Breda, died in a freak accident aged twenty-one.

Brian Lenihan was defeated in the presidential election in 1990 by Mary Robinson, and Mary O'Rourke was very disappointed. She felt her brother who had given loyal service to Charlie Haughey for many years was betrayed by him to save his own skin. I do not know if she had it in her heart to forgive Charlie. Charlie was a survivor and would do anything to stay in power, including sacking his best friend in politics.

PART SIX

1991–2006

THE YEAR 1991 DAWNED AND I HAD TWO formidable new bosses. Noel Lindsay was appointed Secretary General having spent years at the World Bank where he had a huge reputation for dynamic flair, a reputation he fully deserved. Noel had been Assistant Secretary General in 1989 but only for a short period as a stepping-stone to the top job. He had come from a building background and made his name in the Post Primary Building Section as Principal Officer before going to the World Bank. I got on well with him because of our similar backgrounds—he was decent, honest and straight but a hard taskmaster and I had a huge respect for him. He was responsible for the promotion of Michael O'Neill to the post of Assistant Secretary General, part of whose responsibility was Primary Buildings. He had earned a huge but fearsome reputation as an accountant in the Department and part of his new brief was to rein in overspending in my area. Frankly, I did not get on well with him and I was furious when he brought a member of his accounts staff to my section and put her in my payments section without telling me. Seeing his plan, I put her in a mainstream section but Mr. O'Neill rescinded my action. To be fair to the girl, she was a hard-working officer and was loyal to me and we later became good friends. But I was wary about the circumstances in which she was transferred to my payments section. In all my years in service, I never did anything untoward or improper but I felt strongly that an unwarranted stranglehold was being put on my operation. Because of my reputation for overspending, maybe this new regime was needed but it made me less than happy.

The local elections were due in June 1991 and Mary O'Rourke told me not be concerned about overspending in that year as she had unofficial approval from the Taoiseach that this would be sanctioned. So I took her at her word. When the elections were over, Noel Lindsay called his building Principals up to get us to confirm that we had kept the reins on expenditure during the course of the election. I, though nervous, replied that the Minister had approved an overrun for the year and as a result, there would be an excess of five million pounds on the buildings' subhead at year-end. Noel Lindsay was furious and so was Michael O'Neill who said he knew nothing about it, which indeed he did not as I had not told him. In fact, I rarely referred anything to him when he was my boss in Primary Buildings. In the event, the Department of Finance approved the overrun but gave us dire warnings about keeping within budget in the future. Noel Lindsay took swift and characteristic action and he issued an immediate directive that all major expenditure proposals be submitted to Michael O'Neill for advance approval.

In August 1991, Michael O'Neill got into trouble with the Minister by preventing the provision of essential prefabs in the Dublin area, which were required for schools' opening in September. In accordance with standard practice, I authorised the provision of the prefabs before I went on holidays at the end of July. On learning this, Michael issued a circular to all staff rescinding my instructions. When September arrived there were no prefabs provided and in one case, a class was being taught on the grass outside. The morning of 1 September 1991, at 9:30 AM, the Minister rang me and she was in a fury. She asked me what had happened. Why were her instructions about the necessity of prefabs in September apparently disregarded? I told her that I had authorised the prefabs in the usual way in July but then my instructions were countermanded soon after. "By whom?" she asked and I had no option but to tell her. She told me to go on Century Radio at once and explain the late provision of the accommodation, which I did, bluffing it as well as I could. The Minister later told me I did well. I had not washed any dirty linen in public.

The following day, Noel Lindsay called us all up to seek an explanation. I outlined the position from my point of view and referred to the countermanding circular from Michael O'Neill who then said "What circular?" "Is this it?" I said taking a copy of his directive from my pocket and placing it on the table in front of Noel Lindsay—game, set and match, I thought wryly. "Well," he said. The Minister wanted to see us all in the afternoon and asked me to be present.

The Minister was in a rage as Noel Lindsay, Michael O'Neill, and Noel Montayne from Post-Primary sat opposite to her. She said she was incensed that her instructions were countermanded by somebody who enjoyed greater security of tenure than a politician did. I said my piece, so did Michael O'Neill, and Noel Lindsay did his best to calm things down to such a degree that we got away lightly. And Noel thanked me afterwards for not letting the side down in defending my position.

Michael was technically correct in issuing his circular but the bottom line is that you cannot deprive school children of badly needed accommodation, whatever the financial constraints may be, and at your peril do you ignore the instructions of the Minister of the day.

So the end of 1991 was near and I was more constrained in my activities than I had been before and, to add to my woes, Mary O'Rourke was leaving the Department of Education to become

Minister for Health. As Michael O'Neill typically remarked, "I believe George Rowley is no longer bulletproof." Noel Davern was appointed as Minister in her place and, to say the least, he was different from Mary O'Rourke—in style anyway.

It was Frank Fahey who introduced me to Noel Davern the day he arrived in the Department. Frank, laughing, said to him "This is George Rowley, he is married to a Cork woman." Noel knew my reputation and we got on well together for the few months he was Minister. I sat in on deputations with him and fully briefed him but my relationship with him was not as close as it had been with Mary O'Rourke. The duty of a civil servant is to serve the Minister of the day to the best of his ability and this I tried to do. As Minister, he was particularly committed to the handicapped and the disadvantaged, to the extent of ignoring my advice in pursuit of a pet project. But, in his time in Education, Noel Davern as Minister did nothing improper or untoward.

Charlie Haughey resigned as Taoiseach in early 1992 and the hustings began in Fianna Fáil to elect his successor. Noel Davern was supporting Bertie Ahern against Albert Reynolds. I was in his room one day when he was discussing with Ray Burke on the phone the level of support for Bertie. I got up to leave the room but the Minister beckoned me to remain seated. In the event, Bertie did not have the necessary support and withdrew from the race much to the chagrin of Ray Burke, who had bought a new suit in anticipation of a promotion. Noel Davern used to bring me around in his State car to visit schools with his private secretary, Frank Wyse, and would tell the schools authorities wryly "George has the plans but no money." I had enjoyed working with him but his period in office was too short to enable him to make a significant impact.

When Albert Reynolds came to power he sacked Frank Fahey as Minister of State in Education. Frank was crestfallen— I had a long night with him when he left office and to say he was disillusioned would be an understatement—almost in tears.

Mary O'Rourke was demoted in what was in effect a purge by Reynolds. Seamus Brennan was then appointed Minister for Education and he did not seem to want to get involved at all. For example, he would rarely meet a deputation and if, on occasion, he did, he would talk to them standing up, ushering them out his door after a few minutes. I rarely met him as Minister, a huge change from my days with Mary O'Rourke.

At the time I was beginning to feel acute stress and anxiety about work for no external reason. So after talking to Kathleen about it, I decided to go on sick-leave for a period of three months from June 1992. Doctors are very sympathetic to those suffering from work-related stress so I had no trouble getting a sick-certificate from my GP. I knew this would be the end of my days in Primary Buildings but I no longer had the earlier commitment to it. I spent those three months writing short stories— ten in all—which I never bothered getting typed. They are still in my briefcase at home gathering dust along with the rest of my writings. I went to Listowel Writers' Week in June and had the usual ball and then on to Ventry in August. I returned to work in September 1992 to be called up by Noel Lindsay who said he was transferring me up to Primary Policy under Tom Gillen in my own interest. He was concerned that the pressure in Primary Buildings had been responsible for my health problems. Tom was a decent man but was very cautious, in the traditional mode, and found it hard to delegate. There was hardly any pressure in the new Section, and Tom would feed the work to me sporadically. I was proud of what I achieved in Primary Buildings but I always felt that the top brass did not appreciate my worth. I was glad to leave it behind me, with my honour and integrity intact. The section has now moved to Tullamore and has a huge budget amounting to hundreds of millions and has reverted to the "Rolls Royce" mode of building.

In all my years of almost cavalier overspending and corner-cutting, I had only two audit queries and, as Noel Lindsay said after he was before the Public Accounts Committee, I batted them to kingdom come. I was to work in Primary Policy until January 1993 when I was transferred to Youth Affairs Section where after an initial honeymoon period, I was to face the greatest crisis of official life, a crisis that brought me to the gates of insanity.

Michael O'Neill was my Assistant Secretary General for my first year in Youth Affairs and after the initial honeymoon period it was a torrid time. The work was completely new to me and soon the old insecurities, which I had experienced in Personnel in 1970, came back—this time with a vengeance. I spent the first few weeks getting to know the main players in the youth organisations who were in receipt of grant-aid and who spent a lot of their time vying with each other for money, often competing in the same territory. The budget was funded, in the main, by the national lottery and as it was grant aid there was no prospect of an overrun, thus giving you no flexibility. The annual grant allocations were historically based and there was no scope for new entries. Also, two-thirds of the budget was taken up with salaries and there was great inequality in this respect for youth officers who were doing the same work. Liam Aylward was the Minister of State who replaced Frank Fahey and I got on well with him but, like all Ministers, he did not like bad news. The main objective seemed to be to retain the status quo so changes in the operation were minimal. There was the perk of foreign travel going with the job, mainly to the Council of Europe meetings in Strasbourg or Luxembourg. I went to my first such meeting in Luxembourg in March 1993 and got on well with my European counterparts. There was great social activity after the day's work and I soon made a name for myself as a singer. In the end, I was better known for this than being an effective officer. However, I always acquitted myself adequately as a representative of Ireland and know I never let my country down. We went to Vienna with Liam Aylward to a youth conference in April and, though it went well overall, I was very nervous throughout. You are always on your toes when the Minister is around, although

Liam was easy to get on with. I made a mistake one morning in Vienna though when I entered the Minister for a round-table with youth representatives and the press. When he heard that I had done so, he threatened to pull out and it took all my powers of persuasion to get him to take part in the round table. In the event, the Minister acquitted himself well. I had written a few speeches for the Minister to be delivered in Vienna and, as he was speaking on racism and the dangers of extreme national-ism exactly as I had written it, the Slovenian delegate gave me a wink and a salute. In my two and a half years in Youth Affairs, I spent a lot of time in Strasbourg and Brussels. I always enjoyed Strasbourg where we would stay in the European Youth Centre but I hated Brussels where the EU meetings were usually held. I felt I did not have the knowledge or ability to acquit myself well and always felt demoralised—though I never sold the pass on Ireland's position.

Back home it was the grant allocation time for 1993 and this was always a dogfight between the youth organisations who were competing for the limited funds available. My staff would prepare a computer spreadsheet with the proposed allocations and Michael O'Neill would give it a searching scrutiny and you would certainly have to be on your toes for this. This unnerved me greatly and, by September, with emails flying at me from all directions, my mental health began to wilt. By October I felt that I was under siege and I became convinced that I did not have the ability for the job. I felt in such despair that one day I told Paddy Bennis, the decent Assistant Principal, to take over my duties, which he willingly did. I felt that I had not, other-wise, the support I needed from any side.

I was convinced that I was not able for the job and felt that all the youth organisations were aware of this—though I was on friendly terms with all of them. I wrote speeches for the an-nual conferences for the Minister of State and these always went down well and I mixed with all the youth personnel in the vari-ous social activities. I began to go under with acute paranoia and one day I went to Mary Durack, the staff welfare officer who was as kind as she was practical, to enlist her help. She knew it was not drink and managed to get me a doctor in St. Patrick's Hospital, James's Street, who would be of help to me. And this was to be the turning-point for my drink problem and my psychological disorder. Dr. Matt Murphy, whom I first met in late 1993, was to be my saviour. He was an expert on alcoholism and all its damaging side-effects, some deeply rooted and responsible for the feelings of low self-esteem originating as far back as childhood. At our first consultation, he quickly put me at ease and I poured out my heart and cried tears of relief. I went back to work feeling renewed and back to my tasks with optimism but I still had the low self-esteem and was never fully to get rid of it even under Dr. Murphy's care. I met him weekly and got to the bottom of my problems particularly the childhood origins and the later years when I took to drink. We had discussed my nervous breakdown and what lead to it and even now he is not convinced that I am a manic-depressive that I was first diagnosed as in 1969. He would say, "The jury is still out on that," but he was convinced that I was an alcoholic, though he never saw me drinking, merely from what I had told him. He prescribed new medication for me—Epilem and Respirdel—which I take to this day. They help my mood disorders, help me to sleep, and do not have the side effects of the previous medication.

Then he introduced me to Mara DeLacy, a clinical psychologist at the hospital who was responsible for my present state of recovery, along with Dr. Murphy. At our first meeting she promised that she would make me happy, something I clearly was not at that point. She had a successful programme for people who had a difficult childhood, ACOA, an acronym for adult children of dysfunctional families. I made no apologies for saying that I come from a dysfunctional family no matter who it offends. The incidences of nervous disorder in the family prove this beyond doubt. I went to weekly sessions with Mara and, with her and the group's help, I began to peel away the onion-layers and get to the root of my problems, including my alcoholism. There were non-alcoholics in the group as well who were as deeply trauma-tised as I was. I have one good friend from that group and I meet her regularly. I really enjoyed the sessions with Mara and, cou-pled with the regular visits to Dr. Murphy, I was getting into a better frame of mind with the help and support of Mary Durack who assured me lack of knowledge is not stupidity.

At the beginning of 1994, Jack O'Brien took over from Michael O'Neill as my boss and I got on better with him—he left me to my own initiative and did not interfere much. There was a change of government in 1994 as well when the Rainbow Coalition under John Bruton came to power. Bernard Allen was then appointed Minister of State with responsibility for Youth Affairs and he brought in Tom Daly from Cork VEC as his per-sonal advisor. Tom was an expert on youth affairs. The new Minister was more hands on than Liam Aylward was and kept me on my toes backed up by Tom Daly's expertise in the youth area. Despite the psychological help I was getting, I still had deep feelings of inadequacy though, in the main, there were no personnel difficulties. In that period, Denis Healy, Head of Per-sonnel, would come to me regularly and offer me early retire-ment—with added years. He was careful to point out I would nearly get a full pension. He had all the figures worked out when he first made the offer and I was first inclined to jump at it but said I would have to discuss it with my wife before making a decision. Kathleen, in her usual forthright manner, was totally against it. She said I was far too young to retire—I was still only fifty—and that the gratuity would be gone in jig-time. I have always believed in consent in a marriage and reluctantly agreed with Kathleen, though I thought retirement would be the solu-tion to my mental problems. I went back to Denis and told him that I was not accepting the offer. Despite my doubts at the time, I am glad that I did not go at that time and I was to wait another ten years, when I retired at a time of my own choosing with my dignity and integrity intact. When I retired eventually in 2004,

I had over forty years' service which entitled me to a full pension and a massive gratuity, far more than I would have got if I had retired ten years earlier. Kathleen was wise and right and though I was suffering in Youth Affairs, I knew deep-down that she was right.

However, Denis Healy continued offering me early retirement until he himself retired some years ago, before I actually did. His constant efforts had the effect of reducing my broken confidence further but I held my ground. Kathleen and I feel bitter about this still. After all, it was the Department that wanted me in the first place when it thought I would be of use. So I soldiered on in Youth Affairs, dealing with the national situation and going abroad regularly to conferences, holding well the official line.

I went to a Minister's conference with Bernard Allen and Tom Daly to Luxembourg in June and the speech I wrote for the Minister was well-received. The Minister had brought the spreadsheet for the 1994 allocations with him and I went through it with him and Tom Daly in dread that he would reduce my figures, particularly from the point of view of a youth organisation when I had promised, under pressure, a certain sum. But the Minister did not like that organisation. In the event he did not reduce the amount I had proposed though, like all Ministers, he looked after his own constituency. To be fair, some organisations in Cork had been historically underfunded and the Minister was merely making up for this.

Austin Mallon, who was private secretary to this Minister and previous ones, was always a great support to me. He had previously worked in Primary Buildings with me and was very able. The umbilical chord of loyalty had always been there for me in Primary Buildings, especially when I most needed it. I was helped in no small measure in that I knew the work inside out, having done it in all my grades in the service over the years. But Youth Affairs was completely new terrain to me and in my time there I always had the deeply-rooted fear that I was not performing adequately. The foreign trips however helped to alleviate an otherwise torrid experience. In 1994, I went to Copenhagen and Paris twice where I had the use of a limousine and I saw all the sights, even going to the opera. In that year too, I had the usual visits to Strasbourg and Brussels. I always brought home duty-free for Kathleen and presents for the children who were now at University, Conor in Maynooth and Fionnuala at Trinity. Kathleen, who did not work while the children were young, got a part-time job, and the money goes some of the way to her frequent foreign travel. She now works in Noreen's old school in Ballymun and is not ready to retire yet. Knowing her, she will probably go on until she is seventy—she is so energetic. She, certainly, is a mainstay for me and I would be in the gutter without her love and support. Certainly I would not have remained sober all these years. I need her but I still have my programme of recovery and I still go to counselling regularly.

I went to Listowel as usual in June 1994 but I had to leave it early to fly from Shannon to Luxembourg for a conference and the psychological shock of this nearly shattered me. On the Sunday of Writers' Week, we have what John B's son Billy calls "The Healing Session" in his bar and it is the highlight of the week with everybody doing a party piece—Billy and I as co-MCs. The morning I had to fly from Shannon, I was unable to be there for Billy Keane's famous Healing Session. But there have been many more since and the event is going from strength to strength.

Naturally John B is sadly missed but his wife Mary is still going strong and is a gracious hostess. It was Gene Yore who drove me to Shannon that morning and he has been going to Listowel for over twenty years now. Gene is a successful journalist with the Dundalk Democrat and writes a regular column for the paper. Other friends from Writer's Week are Sandra McEvoy, Glennis Spray, and Larry Burke who comes every year from Minnesota and his friend Dan and, more recently, Chris Lacey and Kathleen Britz, and her son AJ who is a talented poet, also from America but who have settled here. I am still very friendly with Susan Keating and Carol Kiley from Washington DC, whom I met in Listowel some years ago.

So it was a culture shock when I arrived in Luxembourg in June 1994 and, though I engaged fully in the official business, I was shaken with emotion about Listowel. In the evenings, I would go for a quiet smoke on my own, not wanting to talk to any of my colleagues. I got addicted to cigars in sobriety and, in effect, I replaced one addiction for another and now cannot kick the habit. I would now put nicotine before alcohol.

I went to Ventry in August 1994 and, as I came down to the exit of Hawkins House where I was based, I looked up at my room and thanked God that I would be free for a whole month which was not long in passing. I did not know then but 1995 was to be my last year in Youth Affairs. Bernard Allen was still actively involved in his brief and, while he was courteous to me at all times, I always felt under strain. There was a new Secretary General in the Department, Dr. Don Thornhill, who got the top job beating my boss, Jack O'Brien, into second place and, needless to say, Jack was disappointed. Don Thornhill, while being very exact, did not bother me much always treating me with great courtesy. Part of the reason was I think that he was a good friend of my brother, Joe, dating back to their days at college. Anyway, Don left me alone and Jack O'Brien was always decent. Denis Healy, a normally gentle, deferential person would still come to me with his old offer but I always refused. I do not blame Denis as there was huge pressure from the Department of Finance to reduce staff numbers. But I knew that I had a contract until I was sixty-five and I was determined that no one would push me until I was good and ready to go.

Then, just before I went on my annual holidays in August 1995, Jack O'Brien called me over to see him and told me in a matter-of-fact way that I was being transferred within a few days. When I asked where to he replied "Archives," and I did not blink an eye. He said, by way of explanation, that there was a lot coming up in Youth Affairs and the Department felt this transfer was in my best interests. I still have a deep feeling that there was something else behind the decision but try as I might I could not find out why I was being moved. I would still retain my grade and salary so what did I care? Deep down though, I knew it was a slap on the wrist but I was not miffed in the least and Archives, where there was no budget, would definitely be quieter than Youth Affairs was.

So I went to my new job having cleared up the files in my room in Hawkins House, where I had such an awful time. I was glad to be rid of the Section regardless of the real circumstances of my departure, which are still a mystery to me. You do what you are told in the Civil Service and you do not ask questions. Over the years, I often thought that I would try to get information about myself through the Freedom of Information Act but I decided to let sleeping dogs lie.

I was to remain in Archives as Principal Officer until the year 2000. Paddy Hickey, a no-nonsense Staff Officer was the driving-force in the section—he had worked his way up through the ranks and did not suffer fools gladly. I have to admit that I did not do myself justice in Archives as I had no computer skills, which were essential for keeping records. So I left most of my work to Paddy Hickey who was thought highly of by the Department. By this stage, my paranoia and anxiety had gone so I started writing poetry and songs, some of which I thought were good. I also wrote a few short stories which were well received in writer's workshops.

In 1996, I went to Gweedore on an Irish Scholarship; I had a great time meeting new friends and singing my new songs as Gaeilge. I went on a similar course in 1997 to Gortahork, and Gweedore again in 1997. I had re-joined the Gaelic League in that period and I had a long-running Irish radio programme on Anna Livia community radio. I would have a different guest on every week and we would discuss topical affairs, all through the medium of Irish. I was Secretary of the Writer's Branch in the

Gaelic League and later Chairman and in that period I organised a number of successful social events. I was also a branch delegate to the annual conference of the Gaelic League three years in succession. I was living a social life to the full and my mental problems had eased considerably although they were not entirely eliminated.

We were still going to Ventry for our annual holidays and I to the Writers' Week in June. All in all I had nothing tangible to worry about, though I was born with a worrying disposition. My head does not sit easily on my shoulders and the slightest upset can throw me. It is a constant battle to keep my equilibrium right but I suppose it will always be like that. Getting the balance right is what I try to achieve and this eluded me until I finally retired in 2004. I am now very content at last.

In 1995, Conor went to America for summer work to West Virginia and I was heart-broken. But he came back in time to go to the All-Ireland final with me which Dublin won. He graduated and did a Higher Diploma in Community and Adult Education and went on to do a Masters in that area. He first started as a teacher but then he got a job working in a Drugs Awareness Programme with the Dublin Archdiocese and worked there for eight years. And, believe it or not, he started recently in the Department of Education as a Youth Work Assessor in my old section, the section that had caused me such grief. I only hope that he is happier there than I was. He recently completed another Masters, this time in psychotherapy, and did well.

Fionnuala went to live in Italy in 2001 and at first Kathleen and I were heartbroken. She is now living there with Simone, her boyfriend, and is very happy. She is a teacher of English and enjoys it and has made a host of new friends all of whom we have met and they are lovely people. Indeed, the Italian connection has opened up a new way of life for all of the family and we visit regularly and the visits are regularly reciprocated by Fionnuala's friends. Conor got married in Riva in 2004 and we had a great if an emotional day, with the pasta and Italian wine flying. I was chuffed when Conor asked me to sing which I did with great pride. I was very nervous however, in the days leading up to the wedding and I thought that I would drink but I did not and my speech went down well. The glorious weather made the whole affair truly wonderful. Conor and Ashley's son was born in August 2005 and he was baptised in December in a little church in Cinegia, near where Fionnuala lives. He was christened Finn Conall and he is the great joy of our lives and Fionnuala dotes on him, being his godmother. Fionnuala lives in the village of Dro, near the city of Riva Del Garda, where the huge cigars are dirt-cheap and the ice cream and coffee are out of this world. Kathleen and I really love Italy, the weather for me in Summer being a particular attraction. Swimming in Lake Garda is an exhilarating experience except that the beach is very rocky and you could cut your feet easily. I love sitting by the lake, smoking a big cigar, and contemplating the Universe. You could work out the square root of minus one in this idyllic ambience. Kathleen loves eating out where the food is very inexpensive and there is a wide range of wines to choose from, also inexpensive. I love it in Summer with the weather a tolerable thirty degrees but it is really cold in winter, sub-zero most of the time. We still go to Ventry as it is our favourite holiday spot and Paud Quinn always gives us a great welcome. It has everything going for it but the weather is often unreliable.

In the year 2000, Denis Healy again offered me early retirement, which I refused, and then told me I was being transferred to Strategic Policy Section under Deirdre O'Keeffe. Deirdre was a hardworking and ambitious Director of policy—she would usually come in at seven in the morning and often work until ten at night. She treated me civilly but was very demanding, wanting everything at once. The work was completely new to me, which brought on my usual feelings of insecurity but they were not as bad as they were in Youth Affairs. I never had occasion to meet the Minister and there were few Parliamentary Questions. I was in charge of paying grants for disadvantaged second-level schools and grants to the Abbey and Team Theatre which I enjoyed very much. I am still very friendly with the staff of Team Theatre who invite me to all their performances. John Dennehy was now Secretary General of the Department having zoomed to the top from the Inspectorate and the Minister was Michael Woods, then Noel Dempsey. I felt that Policy Section was too abstract for me to get to grips with and my experience did not lend itself to the work. For some reason, Deirdre O'Keeffe stopped sending me policy work and I had only now to concentrate on the grants for which I had a budget of two million euro, small fare indeed compared to Primary Buildings. Crucially, you could not overspend but I always found some room for flexibility in my allocations of grants, mostly to the needy. At the end of the year, I always had a bit left over to give to the most disadvantaged which I enjoyed doing. I did not mind being left out of Policy work but it was typical of the Department not to tell me the reasons for this.

The Department's Legal section was also in the Policy building and, though I had no official dealings with the staff there, I was on friendly terms with them all. I did most of my work by email but never quite mastered it. One of the main disadvantages of Policy and Archives Sections was that there was no travel whatsoever. This was a huge shock to me after Primary Buildings where I travelled the length of the country and Youth Affairs where I went Europe frequently. But I did not mind, though I would have welcomed the expenses. I was quite comfortable on a Principal's salary with Kathleen working part-time as well.

Then Deirdre O'Keeffe was promoted to CERT, a semi-state body and she was replaced by Tom Boland, a barrister, as Director. He was a decent, kind and hardworking man and left me to my own devices. He was fully occupied on legal matters where there were almost daily court cases. There was another Principal Officer now on Strategic Policy and it soon became evident to me that I was to concentrate on the disadvantaged grants; something I thought I was good at. Tom was to be my last boss and he let me get on with my job with which I was not overstretched. I was gradually easing my way into retirement, though there would always be the odd moments of anxiety for me.

In 2003, having discussed the matter with Kathleen, I made up my mind to retire in January 2004 with almost forty-one years service, having reached my sixtieth birthday the previous September. There were some pay increases due and I wanted to boost my lump sum to the maximum possible. I could have remained at work until I was sixty-five but, because it was now a changed atmosphere in the Civil Service, I decided to go while I was still in good health. I was also going at a time of my own choosing, which was important to me, and I felt I was not being pushed which was also crucial. So the time was right, I thought, and I have no regrets whatsoever. The lump sum was substantial and I have invested it wisely and have no debts. I own my own house now—not bad for someone who was so profligate. But I owe it all to Kathleen, without her my finances would not be so rosy. I have half-pay, which is the equivalent of the salary of a Higher Executive Officer, and I can get by on it as I have few needs. My only luxuries are cigars, going to the movies and the theatre, and holidays to Listowel, Ventry and Italy. But I am satisfied with my lot.

Coming to retirement day, the big question for me was whether I would have a presentation. At first, I thought I would confine it to the Section but, as the day got nearer, I was prevailed upon my colleagues to have a bigger presentation than I had first intended. So about a fortnight before the event I sent an email to all staff inviting them along on 16 January 2004. As the day drew near I cleared my desk without regret, almost without feeling, and packed all my private papers into a crate, which included all my creative writings, mostly untyped. I left no official work undone and I cleared all my emails and turned off my computer for the last time.

I was invited down to Tullamore by my old Buildings colleagues for a going-away party and we sat well into the night talking about old times. I knew that I had earned their respect and it was good, though sad, to see all the old faces who had soldiered with me through thick and thin.

I was very nervous the morning of the formal presentation, 16 January 2004, as I was afraid I would drink. But I got Brian Kerneghen, a new friend, to mind me for the morning. What I was most afraid of was that something would come out of the woodwork which would embarrass me, Kathleen or Conor who were also coming to the presentation. Breda Naughton, a lovely lady, made the arrangements and I bought drink in the nearby Dunnes Stores. My colleagues started drifting in at about three o'clock and then old faces from the OPW, which surprised me, because I had not told them of the event but I was glad to see them. Martin Hanevy, Assistant Secretary General was the first speaker, with Tom Boland and Maura O'Flaherty who worked with me in Primary Buildings; Joe Fahey spoke and was very eloquent and said we always did the right thing. Then Tom Sherlock, a union colleague from the OPW, spoke of my union activities when he said I always put principle first often at the expense of my career. This pleased me greatly as it did Conor who had never known of my union activities. Most of the speakers spoke of my creative writing and entertainment interests but not one of them mentioned my official career or Primary Buildings. Although there was no Minister present, I did receive a fax from Mary O'Rourke headed "A Tribute to George Rowley" where she recalled the ground-breaking days in buildings which pleased Kathleen very much. Though at first I thought the speeches were patronising, Conor and my friends assured me that they were not. Conor was very pleased and Kathleen was presented with a bouquet of flowers. I received a print, a voucher for a holiday in Parknasilla and numerous book tokens. I thought the whole thing went well and I made a dignified speech saying my piece, without emotion, but not wanting to embarrass anyone. I relaxed at the party in the Office and at the end of it we went to Briody's pub nearby where I had hired a room for the rest of the evening. So I left the office for the last time with relief but not with any regret. I knew that I had had a good career and was effective in most grades in which I had served in both the OPW and the Department. In Briodys, I felt I had left a legacy and I felt proud, as did my family. That is all that mattered to me.

We had a hectic night in Briodys, almost hilarious, and I bought a good few rounds. Kathleen's sisters, Mary and Esther, arrived but Conor and Ashley had to leave for a while to attend a pre-marriage course. Joe Boland was there with his daughter, Anne, now a senior civil servant. Joe had a tragedy a few years ago when his son died and he never got over it. Joe, at the best of times, is almost on the morose side but he is a good friend. He is retired now and I meet him and Joe Fahey occasionally. During the course of the evening, I took a break and went downstairs for a few smokes—Barry Harte, a friend of mine, had given me a packet of magnificent Cuban cigars for the occasion—and I sat on my own, taking in the world, reflecting on the whole evening and my life. I puffed and reflected and felt good.

I have no regrets about leaving the Service when I did. Doubtless I had some achievements and, despite my despair at times which seemed unending, I never let the side down. I was rooted to the floor with fear and paranoia, often puking, but I always went to work. I feel that that was courageous of me. Only Kathleen knows the depth of my insecurities and I know that she ensured my survival. I look forward to a tranquil old age with her and my children and grandchild. I have very few ambitions left—I want to live as long as possible, Kathleen too, in peace and harmony and to have good health. Life can be cruel—you can be cut-down in an instant. I next want to become an established writer and I want it to be quality writing, subject only to my limitations, of which I am always conscious. If you exceed your limitations, you will eventually turn to drink or drugs, which will destroy you. I spent far too long abusing myself and burning that talent which was death to hide (Milton – *On His Blindness*). So I now vow to have a real go and find out whether I have what it takes. I want to be published and I want to have an impact on my readers who might say "I know what he feels," even after I am dead and gone. Though I know I am loved by my family and friends, I want them to appreciate me as a writer. But it is up to me to take action, apart from the writing. I need to get my stuff typed and try to get it published else I will have failed to exploit my talents, however limited.In retirement, I have read a lot at Fionnuala's urging and have now read all Paul Auster's work—he is a writer from Brooklyn, USA and I would strongly recommend him. I have read a lot of biographies and just before I started writing this memoir, such as it is, I read all John Steinbeck's letters—a prodigious output. His accounts of his early days of failure being particularly encouraging in a perverse way. If the great Steinbeck had his struggles, should I, a mere amateur, be an exception?

In writing this memoir I have tried to be honest, within the constraints of prudence and dangers of libel. I left a lot out and was careful not to criticise people who are still alive, although they might have wronged me on the road to now. However, despite this, I may have hurt people, especially my wider family, and I am sorry for that. But I had a duty to put all I actually said on the record, a testament, as it were, to my upbringing, my career and my life generally. In doing so I hope I am forgiven for any lapses or shortcomings in my memory which is often a tricky and unreliable facility.

I have had, overall, a good life and I am grateful to Providence for persevering with me, a flawed soul. When I come to the end of my tenure there is nothing I will not have tried, within the constraints of propriety. There will be no ifs, buts or maybes; I will have given life my best shot when the Lord calls me to account. He is the final arbiter and I have no fears about the death which awaits me, later than sooner I hope; this is my fervent wish.

Joy

And when joy comes,
It comes quickly.
It is effusive and overwhelming.
The pain of yesterday is behind the locked door of the past.
Joy at last.
Incipient negativity
is brushed aside with glee.
Let joy now carry me
on its ecstatic wave.
All is now possible
That seemed impossible.
I will write that letter.
We will walk together in Summer
And view the red ball of the sun,
Laced with soft grey
and maybe talk 'til dawn
The harbinger of all hope.
I will share with her
Things locked in my head
And won't feel foolish.
Shouts between workmen no longer rankle.
The chimes from church steeples
Seem in tune with my heart.
I tousled a child's curls just now.
His mother seemed to understand.
And I saw a pigeon picking at a crisp
And I realised
I value life
And always did.
And joy has come.
Will it last?
Negativity again.
But I fasten on to now
It is all we have

George Rowley

BIOGRAPHICAL DETAILS

Born Dublin, 1943.

Educated at Stanhope Street Convent, O'Connell School and University College Dublin. Served in the Office of Public Works from 1963–1985 and the Department of Education and Science from 1985–2004. Retired in January 2004 and now intends to devote himself fulltime to creative writing.

Married with a son, a daughter and one grandson.